INSIGHT COMPACT GUIDE

Las

CW00321835

Compact Guide: Las Vegas is the ultimate quick-reference guide to this exuberantly escapist city. It tells you all you'll need to know about Las Vegas's attractions, from the glamour and glitz of the celebrated casinos on The Strip and the nightly neon shows pulling in the crowds Downtown to the incomparable white-heat excursions deep into the high desert.

This is one of 130 Compact Guides, combining the interests and enthusiasms of two of the world's best-known information providers: Insight Guides, whose innovative titles have set the standard for visual travel guides since 1970, and Discovery Channel, the world's premier source of nonfiction television programming.

APA PUBLICATIONS
Part of the Langenscheidt Publishing Group

Insight Compact Guide: Las Vegas

Written by: John Wilcock
Photography by: Glyn Genin
Additional photography by: Las Vegas Convention
and Visitors Authority/Las Vegas News Bureau
Cover Picture: D&J Heaton
Picture Editor: Hilary Genin
Cartographic Editor: Maria Donnelly
Design Concept: Carlotta Junger

Editorial Director: Brian Bell
Managing Editor: Martha Ellen Zenfell

CONTACTING THE EDITORS: As every effort is made to provide accurate information in this publication, we would appreciate it if readers would call our attention to any errors and omissions by contacting:
Apa Publications, PO Box 7910, London SE1 1WE, England.
Fax: (44 20) 7403 0290
e-mail: insight@apaguide.demon.co.uk

Information has been obtained from sources believed to be reliable, but its accuracy and completeness, and the opinions based thereon, are not guaranteed.

© 2002 APA Publications GmbH & Co. Verlag KG Singapore Branch, Singapore.

First Edition 1996. Second Edition 2002
Printed in Singapore by Insight Print Services (Pte) Ltd

Distributed in the United States by:
Langenscheidt Publishers, Inc.
46–35 54th Road, Maspeth, NY 11378
Tel: (1 718) 784-0055, Fax: (1 718) 784-0640

Distributed in the UK & Ireland by:
GeoCenter International Ltd
The Viables Centre, Harrow Way, Basingstoke,
Hampshire RG22 4BJ
Tel: (44 1256) 817-987, Fax: (44 1256) 817-988

Worldwide distribution enquiries:
APA Publications GmbH & Co. Verlag KG (Singapore Branch)
38 Joo Koon Road, Singapore 628990
Tel: (65) 865-1600, Fax: (65) 861-6438

www.insightguides.com

Las Vegas

Introduction

Places

Culture

Travel Tips

△ **Paris Las Vegas (p39)** Vive la France with fun cafés on Le Boulevard and a half-size scale model of the Eiffel Tower.

▽ **Stratosphere Tower (p63)** Sample the best views in Vegas in an ear-popping 30-second ride.

▷ **The Venetian (p44)** *Gondolieri* on the Grand Canal, a Guggenheim Museum and the largest spa in Vegas make the Venetian one of the classiest stops on The Strip.

▽ **The Mirage (p47)** Volcanoes erupt nightly, but magicians and tigers are the real attractions in the Mirage's popular Siegfried & Roy Show.

△ **Fremont Street Experience (p65)** Under no circumstances miss this spectacular, overhead moving picture show which takes place hourly and spans five city blocks Downtown.

△ **Cirque du Soleil (p50** and **p53)** Choose between two excellent, permanent shows, but be sure to book in advance.

△ **The Luxor (p30)** Hieroglyphics, green laser beams, a pyramid and a Sphinx form just part of this huge 30-story, glass-paneled casino-hotel.

▽ **Hoover Dam (p77)** This enormous dam straddles two states and is an awesome sight to see.

△ **The Bellagio (p52)** Water, water everywhere is the theme of this lavish palace in the desert, named for a town on Lake Como in Italy.

▷ **New York, New York (p18)** Visitors can walk in Central Park or ride a Coney Island-style roller coaster here.

Diamond in the Desert

Las Vegas sits in the Nevada desert surrounded by absolutely nothing, a neon jewel in the emptiness. As Aaron Betsky, an architect turned writer who designed some of the city's earliest casinos, says: 'There is not much logic to Las Vegas. There are no natural resources and nothing is close by. This is what has allowed the city to become an outlaw place of escape.'

Las Vegas feeds off dreams. People come to dream of getting rich, to dream for a few days that they are rich, and to forget the commonplace, everyday world. It's a fantasy world where everything seems possible, where you truly can get something for nothing. Las Vegas sells its visitors the most powerful of opiates: here, your life could radically change in the next five minutes.

This is a town where a single hotel costs more to build than the Hoover Dam, one of the seven modern wonders of the world just a short drive away, but also a town where people can get a room, food and drinks for free as long as they gamble enough. Paradoxically, there is one guaranteed way to win in Las Vegas. If you don't gamble, it's one of the world's cheapest vacation spots. Hotel rooms for as little as $17 and steak dinners for $4.99 are hard to beat.

Nevada's gaming revenue is almost $8 billion annually, and 90 percent of this astonishing sum comes from Clark County and Las Vegas, with most of that coming from slot machines. Even the nickel slots earn the casinos a scarcely credible $1 billion each year.

> **What's in a name?**
> The phrase 'las vegas' means 'the meadows' in Spanish. It refers to ancient underground springs in the desert, near the site of the present city, that from time to time produced an oasis.

Opposite: gondolieri *at the Venetian Hotel*
Below: welcome to sun, fun and illusion

LOCATION AND SIZE

Situated in Clark County in Nevada's southeast corner, Las Vegas accounts for about one-third of the county's 1.32 million population, and this is increasing rapidly each year. Nevada, the seventh largest state in the US by area, is now the 32nd most populated, having almost 2 million residents; the number of retired people is increasing

four times as fast as in the rest of the US. For four decades in a row, Nevada has been the fastest-growing state in America.

CLIMATE

Nevada receives an average of four inches (10cm) of rainfall a year, with more than 250 days of sunshine. Summers are hot, with temperatures frequently exceeding 100°F (40°C); in winter, temperatures can be a pleasant 65°F (18°C), but night times are cold. Early spring and late fall are the best times to visit, as days are warm and nights comfortably cool.

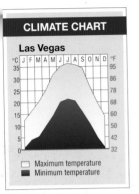

CLIMATE CHART

Las Vegas

☐ Maximum temperature
■ Minimum temperature

A city with an insatiable thirst

ENERGY AND EDUCATION

Las Vegas, a vast consumer of energy, receives most of its water from Hoover Dam, located on the Nevada/Arizona border. The energy crisis which hit the state of California in 2001 has also affected this glittering city in the desert, and as fuel costs rise, some of these charges have been passed on to the consumer, in the form of hotel surcharges. Solar power and geothermal energy (which harnesses heat from beneath the earth's surface) are being investigated as necessary alternatives to existing energy sources.

Unfortunately, despite its popularity as a place to live, the state gets poor grades for the health and well-being of its residents, ranking 44th out of 50 in a recent study conducted by a charity. Nevada, the report concluded, has higher rates of teen dropouts and pregnancies, and more low income families than most of the rest of the country.

CASINO SCHOOL

Nevada has no franchise tax, inventory tax or corporate income tax, and about three-quarters of the billions lost in the casinos are left right there in the city. Las Vegas tourism and gambling are the two major employers, and they require internal investment, not to mention training. At the

Community College of Southern Nevada, where students attend classes in the casino lab equipped with roulette wheels, slot machines, video surveillance systems and blackjack tables, simulated casino noise is piped in for atmosphere, and cheaters and card counters are in attendance to keep the students alert.

The professors, all of whom are longtime gaming industry professionals, teach gaming regulations and the theory of odds. Koreans who want to be trained to work at casinos in their homeland can attend classes in their own language.

BEFORE THE GAMBLERS

For serious or merely curious students of local history, the Las Vegas Natural History Museum and the Nevada State Museum cover a lot of ground, with the latter exhibiting a life-sized skeleton of a Columbian mammoth which was accidentally uncovered by construction workers. This huge beast, hidden for centuries, roamed the area at least 8,000 years ago, before prehistoric southern Nevada evolved from a virtual marsh to the parched, arid landscape that could support only the hardiest of plants and animals. This landscape is virtually timeless, as a visit to Red Rock Canyon or the Valley of Fire will attest.

Underground water sporadically surfaced to

Below: the prehistoric Valley of Fire State Park
Bottom: the captain ties the knot at Treasure Island

produce the occasional oasis, one of which offered artesian spring water at what came to be called Las Vegas Springs. The spring was discovered in 1829 by the young Mexican scout Rafael Rivera, who was accompanying a trader along the Spanish Trail to Los Angeles.

Below: John C Fremont
Bottom: Bugsy told the story of Las Vegas and the Mob

FREMONT ARRIVES

A few years later, the renowned explorer John C Fremont – his name preserved on a downtown street – camped at the spring, which in 1855 also nurtured the first Mormon settlers who were dispatched by founder Brigham Young. Although they planted orchards and mined lead from the Potosi Mountains, the Mormons eventually abandoned the area due to constant Indian raids.

A remnant of their adobe fort still exists Downtown at the intersection of Las Vegas Boulevard North and Washington Avenue, which is in the process of being recontructed. Meanwhile, their story and that of the Indians, the railroad tycoons and the miners who followed later can be plotted in the Clark County Heritage Museum and the Marjorie Barrick Museum on the University of Nevada-Las Vegas campus.

MOBSTERS MOVE IN

The gambling capital we know today had its origins in the 1940s, when Tommy Hull built the El Rancho Vegas opposite the site of today's Sahara Hotel. In 1945, the mobster Benjamin 'Bugsy' Siegel, a member of the Meyer Lansky crime organization, built the Flamingo Hotel with a giant pink neon sign and pink flamingos on the wall. It opened on New Year's Eve, 1946, but six months later Siegel was murdered by a shotgun blast at his girlfriend's Beverly Hills house. His sudden demise followed allegations that he had been skimming the take.

The success of Warren Beatty's 1992 movie *Bugsy* prompted the hotel (now owned by Hilton) to open the Bugsy Celebrity Theater, but the final authentic reminder of the Siegel era disappeared in December, 1993, when the bullet-proof casino office in which the gangster spent his time was bulldozed.

FEW RESTRICTIONS

There were few restrictions in the early days: no cover charge, no minimum bill, no sales tax, no waiting for marriage licenses, no speed limits. It was also a time when nobody inquired too closely about who was pulling the strings. It was an open secret that the Mob ran Vegas, and that hundreds of thousand of dollars were skimmed off the take every week and shipped by couriers to Chicago. By the 1970s, with Frank 'Lefty' Rosenthal as the Mafia's frontman, things were getting out of hand, and the syndicate destroyed itself from within. Martin Scorsese's 1995 film *Casino* tells the story more or less as it happened.

The arrival of Howard Hughes in 1967 pre-cipitated a major change. His ownership of six casinos, generating about a quarter of Vegas gaming revenues, marked the shift towards cor-porate ownership. Today, under the gaze of a vigilant state gaming authority and tax watch-dogs, the gambling business is squeaky clean. But respectability has brought familiar problems: police reports show an influx of the kind of street gangs seen in almost every major US city. The

Made in Las Vegas
Here are just a few of the movies filmed in whole or in part in Las Vegas:

Ocean's Eleven	1960
Viva Las Vegas	1964
Diamonds are Forever	1971
The Godfather II	1974
Bugsy	1992
Honeymoon in Vegas	1992
Casino	1995
Leaving Las Vegas	1995
Con Air	1997
Fear and Loathing in Las Vegas	1998
The Mexican	2000
Ocean's Eleven (remake)	2001

Sin City in 1950

Washington Post once ran a story suggesting that citizens sometimes yearned for the bad old days. 'Those punks wouldn't have dared show their faces when Bugsy was around,' groused one old-timer.

ENTERTAINMENT FOR ALL

Below and bottom:
Las Vegas's popular pursuits

In the early 1960s, almost all the casinos ran a similiar setup, with headliners such as Frank Sinatra, Sammy Davis Jr and other members of the high-profile, hard-living Hollywood hell-raising group called 'the Rat Pack' performing nightly in the supper clubs. Then, in 1966, Caesars Palace broke Strip convention. The casino's Mediterranean-style grounds, with fountains and statuary, sported life-size fiberglass centurions at the entrance, and its Bacchanal restaurant had wine goddesses offering gentle massages. Two years later, Sarno opened the Circus Circus casino in which aerialists, fire-eaters and jugglers performed while slot machines clattered.

Since then, improvements in the technology and expertise available to the entertainment industries have resulted in shows that would once have been beyond the imagination. With the new spate of gigantic hotels boasting upwards of 5,000 rooms, and building and businesses booming, the city has been taking another quantum leap forward, just as it did in the 1960s.

STATISTICS TO DIE FOR

Corporations love the casino business because the house always wins. Hilton's Nevada casinos bring in more than twice the revenues of all 270 of its franchised hotels worldwide, revenues which in themselves are considerable.

Three local casino operators make *Fortune* magazine's roster of America's largest companies. They are Park Place Entertainment, whose revenues of $4.896 billion earned it 355th place; Harrah's (with $3.471 billion, 470th on the list; and MGM Mirage ($3.232 billion, 496th).

Las Vegas's room occupancy rate of 90 percent (compared with the national rate of around 64 percent), and rising to 94 percent on weekends, in its 125,000 hotel rooms means plenty of would-be gamblers. The average visitor is aged 50 and, spreading his or her time between the city's 70 different casinos, spends $560 on gambling alone.

The statistics keep coming: the year 2000's figure of 35.8 million visitors – about one-tenth attending conventions – was 6 percent more than the previous year, which itself was a 10 percent increase on the year before that. With its 6 million square feet (557,000 square meters) of exhibition and meeting space, Las Vegas has consistently topped the trade-show destination list.

CASTLES IN THE SAND

Las Vegas's transformation in the past 10 years is due mainly to its extraordinary collection of casinos on the Strip. The architects of these fantasy palaces cast their nets wide, drawing on influences as diverse as Egypt, New York, Venice and Paris – not to mention Hollywood and Disneyland. A 'family-friendly' atmosphere has been encouraged, and since the aim of the game is to get people gambling, food and accommodation are inexpensive, sometimes even free.

In fact, Las Vegas is now one of America's cheapest places to take a vacation – as long as you steer clear of the gaming tables.

Wedding bells
Apart from gambling, the thing for which Las Vegas is best known is its marriage business. In a recent year, Las Vegas and the desert city of Laughlin issued between them more than 115,000 marriage licenses. Visitors can be married by Merlin while a fire-breathing dragon attempts to thwart the nuptials; don medieval or intergalactic wedding gear and hire Star Trek characters as their witnesses, or tie the knot in front of an Elvis impersonator. One chapel offers a drive-in marriage window, so eager lovers need not even leave the car.

The Bellagio's fabulous fountains and desert position

HISTORICAL HIGHLIGHTS

1829 Mexican trader Antonio Armijo's party, en route to Los Angeles, discovers springs in the desert and names the land 'Las Vegas.'

1844 John C. Fremont, leading an overland expedition west, camps at Las Vegas Springs on a site that later bears his name, Fremont Street.

1848 The US acquires the region after winning the Mexican War.

1855 Mormon settlers build an adobe fort to fortify and protect the mail route from Los Angeles, California, to Salt Lake City, Utah.

1859 Discovery of the gold- and silver-rich Comstock Lode makes millionaires out of publisher tycoon William Randolph Hearst and others.

1864 Nevada is admitted into the Union during the Civil War.

1905 The San Pedro, Los Angeles and Salt Lake Railroad (later to become the Union Pacific) makes an inaugural run and auctions lots in a new town called Las Vegas.

1911 The city of Las Vegas is formally incorporated.

1926 Western Airlines makes its first commercial flight into Las Vegas.

1931 The Legislature approves a gambling bill authored by rancher Phil Tobin to raise taxes for public schools. Construction begins on the Hoover Dam in Black Canyon.

1935 President Franklin Roosevelt dedicates Hoover Dam. The dam's generators produce enough electricity for all.

1940 Las Vegas's population is 8,422. Clark County, in which it is located, has a population of 16,414 people.

1941 Tommy Hull builds El Rancho Vegas on land opposite today's Sahara Hotel. El Cortez Hotel opens Downtown.

1942 The Last Frontier Hotel opens, later to be called the Frontier.

1945 The mobster Benjamin 'Bugsy' Siegel, a member of the Meyer Lansky crime organization, opens the Flamingo Hotel. He is murdered six months later, allegedly because he was 'skimming the take.' The state levies the first gaming taxes, which boost Nevada's economy.

1950 Las Vegas's population is 64,624; Clark County's is 48,289.

1955 The 9-story Riviera Hotel becomes the city's first high rise. The Moulin Rouge opens with former heavyweight champion boxer Joe Louis as a co-owner, but black entertainers are obliged to live off the premises. Nevada legislature creates the Gaming Control Board.

1959 The Nevada Gaming Commission is created by order of the state legislature, to keep an eye on illegal activities. The first Las Vegas Convention Center opens.

1960 El Rancho Vegas burns down.

1966 The reclusive millionaire Howard Hughes moves into a penthouse on top of the Desert Inn. His six casinos mark the beginning of a move from private to corporate ownership.

1967 Nevada's legislature allows publicly traded corporations to obtain gambling licenses.

1975 Nevada gaming revenues top $1 billion.

1980 Las Vegas (population 164,674) celebrates its 75th birthday.

1989 The Mirage casino opens with 3,039 rooms.

1990 Las Vegas's population reaches 258,295.

1992 Warren Beatty's successful movie *Bugsy* prompts the Flamingo Hilton to open the Bugsy Celebrity Theater. Nevada aggressively pursues Hollywood film studios and in the 1990s, films with a Las Vegas backdrop become a common sight on the silver screen.

1993 The Dunes' owner, Steve Wynn, demolishes Bugsy Siegel's office for a new resort. Treasure Island and The Luxor open. The MGM Grand opens as the world's biggest resort.

1994 Downtown's Fremont Street is closed to traffic as work begins on the Fremont Street Experience. Pedestrian skywalks are built over the intersection of Tropicana Boulevard and the Strip. Nonstop regular charter services from Europe begin.

1995 Clark County's population tops 1 million. Clark County casino gaming revenues are $5.7 billion – 78 percent of the US total. A $25 million monorail runs between the MGM Grand and Bally's, on the east side of the Strip. The Fremont Street Experience opens.

1996 Stateline, on the California border, is renamed Primm, in honor of its founder Ernest Primm. Singer Wayne Newton celebrates his 25,000th Las Vegas performance. Entertainers Siegfried and Roy celebrate their 15,000th Las Vegas performance. The first tunnel under the Strip is completed. The Monte Carlo and the Stratosphere Tower both open on the Strip, and the Tropicana celebrates its 40th birthday.

1997 On the site of the former Sands Hotel, ground is broken to build the Venetian Hotel and Resort. The old Aladdin Hotel closes to make way for the construction of a new 17-story 'Moroccan fantasy.' New York-New York opens, initially welcoming 100,000 visitors a day among whom is a local, Sue Henley, who wins $12.5 million – the largest slot-machine jackpot in history.

1998 The respected old Aladdin Hotel is imploded. Both Northwest and Japan Airlines inaugurate nonstop service from Tokyo to Las Vegas, and Korean Airlines operates charter flights from Seoul. The Bellagio, billed as the most expensive hotel in the world ($1.7 billion), opens with a policy banning persons under 18 who are not registered guests. The Debbie Reynolds hotel-casino is sold at public auction to the World Wrestling Federation for $9.27 million. A 66-year-old local resident wins a $27 million progressive Megabucks jackpot at the Palace Station Hotel Casino.

1999 The Mandalay Bay Resort opens. MGM Grand buys its across-the-street neighbor, New York-New York. Paris Las Vegas opens, with a replica of the Eiffel Tower. Singer Barbra Streisand receives a reputed $1 million for one night's work, to inaugurate the new-century celebrations on New Year's Eve.

2000 The Venetian opens with over 3,000 suites, which it expects to double with a second building phase to make it the world's largest hotel. MGM Grand creates the largest corporate buyout in gaming history with its purchase of Mirage Resorts Inc. Nevada gives its approval for the Strip monorail.

1: Crossroads of the World

New York-New York – Monte Carlo – Tropicana – MGM Grand – Grand Canyon

3700–3800 Las Vegas Boulevard (The Strip)

Map on page 20

Top for tips

The *Las Vegas Advisor* is probably the best local source for unbiased information and tips about bargains, because its reporters pay their own way to check things out. 'Sometimes casinos send us comps and we send them a check in return, leaving the payee's line blank,' says editor Deke Castleman. 'That lets us see which casinos cash them in and which turn them over to charity.'

Preceding pages: night-time on The Strip
Below: Crossroads of the World

The 'Crossroads of the World' is traversed by as many as a quarter of a million cars a day. At least 36 million visitors came to Las Vegas in the year 2000, a 62 percent increase over the figure for 1990 – and sometimes it seems they are all on the Strip at the same time. Nowhere is this more so than its meeting with Sahara Avenue, where the casinos representing both the East Coast of America (New York-New York) and the West Coast (MGM Grand) make up the busiest crossroads in the world.

More than 50,000 pedestrians ride up and down the elevators, escalators and elevated pedestrian crossways that interconnect at this busy corner. At New York-New York, visitors can admire the world's most famous skyline and visit cloned landmarks such as the Statue of Liberty, the 47-story Empire State Building and the Brooklyn Bridge. The other corners of this crossroads are occupied by the Tropicana and the white spires of the Disney-style Excalibur *(see page 32)*, a medieval castle with moat and drawbridge resembling, according to one comic, 'a penitentiary for Snow White.'

NEW YORK-NEW YORK

Opened in January 1997, the 47-story ★★★ **New York-New York ❶** hotel and casino, at 529ft (161 meters) the state's tallest, brought the former mayor of New York, Ed Koch, and a Sinatra lookalike to the ground-breaking ceremony. Long before the hotel opened, over 2,000 rooms were filled by previewers reveling in the appeal of staying in the Big Apple without actually having to go there. Visitors can walk in Central Park, cross a 300-ft (90-meter) Brooklyn Bridge, ride the Manhattan Express, a Coney Island-style roller coaster, and stroll along a graffitied Lower East Side-type street of shops and eateries, where

Broadway improbably intersects Sheridan Square and Greenwich Street. New York-New York achieved even greater fame later in its opening year when a local construction inspector named Sue Henley won $12.5 million on the slot machines.

'The interesting thing to me about New York-New York,' says University of Nevada professor Dave Hickey, 'is that visually, externally it really is a successful building. It solves the façade problem by multiplying façades (which also) solves the scale problem.' The exterior is better than the interior, but inside there *is* a Krispy Kreme outlet so beloved of New Yorkers, and an ESPN Sports Bar with 12-foot screens. Around the premises are another 160 TV monitors, of which a dozen are in the washrooms. New York-New York is one of seven casinos operated around the country by the Disney Company.

Monte Carlo

Next door to New York-New York, the ★★ **Monte Carlo ❷**, operated by the Mandalay Resorts Group, features its own brew pub, whose giant copper tanks and industrial design share space with restaurants and old-fashioned gas lamps on its period-style Street of Dreams. Its interior designer, Terry Dougall, was also responsible for the much-lauded Forum Shops by Caesars Palace,

Star Attraction
● New York-New York
● Monte Carlo

Below: Monte Carlo
Bottom: New York-New York

Map
below

and worked on the Venetian as well as the immense Mandalay Bay Hotel-Casino; this last gives an idea of the major future expansion of the Strip to the south, past the Luxor, where Mandalay Resorts Group owns almost one mile of frontage.

Starring since 1996 at the Monte Carlo is the longtime Vegas headliner, the amiable Lance Burton, the city's top magician. Burton spent his money at the magic shop as a kid, getting some back by doing shows and charging a 5¢ admission. He took on an eight-week gig at the Las Vegas version of Folies Bergeres, stayed for nine years, and then moved his show to the Hacienda; he was also watched by millions on TV's *The Tonight Show*.

Lance Burton, magician at the Monte Carlo

THE LEGENDARY DUNES HOTEL

The Monte Carlo stands on the site of the legendary Dunes Hotel (famous during 'the Rat Pack' days of the 1950s, when high-profile party-goers like Frank Sinatra, Dean Martin and Sammy Davis, Jr performed in Vegas clubs and chased girls behind the scenes, raising the profile and lowering the tone of the city simultaneously).

Modern property developer Steve Wynn bought the Dunes for $75 million and then spent another $1.5 million demolishing it. He linked the Monte Carlo by monorail to the adjoining Bellagio (now owned by MGM Mirage).

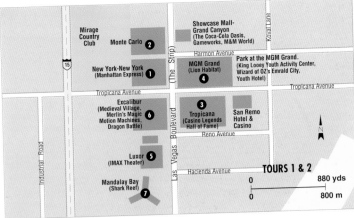

It had been the Dunes, back in 1957, that introduced topless showgirls to the Strip with Minsky's Follies, thus inaugurating a showgirl style. This was followed successfully by the Stardust, which imported the 'Lido de Paris' from France for a run that lasted 31 years.

THE TROPICANA

Since 1959, the showgirl tradition has been maintained by 25,000 performances of the Folies Bergeres at the ★★ **Tropicana** ❸, which visitors can sometimes preview on an afternoon tour. The tours are often conducted by a statuesque lead dancer called Linda who, at 6ft (2 meters) tall and 108 lbs (49 kg), claims to be overweight. The tour takes participants backstage to see the hundreds of heavily weighted cables, all numbered and identified, that are operated by 'flymen' who can't see the show, but who raise and lower the sets according to musical cues. An ancient silver Chevy with FOLIES on the license plate sits at the side of the stage ready for its brief appearance.

The tour proceeds past a sign requesting that 'All male performers please knock before entering', and through dressing rooms littered with sequined costumes, wigs and feathered fans. Personal items, flowers and photographs sit on dressing tables. Each dancer has half a dozen pairs of $150 shoes. These glamorous 'girls' make around $40,000 a year, but there is lots of potential for $20-per-hour jobs at conventions, handing out literature, pushing buttons and the like. 'I had to demonstrate a video golf game and I don't even play,' says Linda. 'Did you have to do it naked?' asks a voice from the group.

SHOWGIRL TRADITION

The Folies Bergeres, born in Paris in 1869, was brought to the Tropicana in 1959 by Lou Walters, the father of ABC's Barbara Walters. However, the first foreign dancers to appear in Las Vegas had arrived the year before, with the opening of the Stardust. Producers such as Lou Walters and

★

Star Attraction
● The Tropicana

Rogues Gallery
Among the exhibits in the Tropicana's Casino Legends Hall of Fame is a sample page from the secret Black Book. The Black Book contains pictures and background about known gamblers of 'notorious or unsavory reputation' who are banned from various casinos.

The Tropicana village

Map on page 20

Donn Arden, whose dance group performed at the Desert Inn, didn't hire girls under 5 feet 8 inches (1.7 meters) tall. Today, the classic showgirl must still be tall, ultra thin and poised, although dancers may be slightly shorter than before, and clothed.

In the 1960s, when the showgirls had finished performing, they were still required to do what was politely called 'mixing.' This entailed sitting with high rollers and maybe gambling with them. The practice died in the early 1970s, when hotels stopped catering exclusively to big spenders and began to target small-time dollar gamblers.

Below and bottom: the two sides of Vegas

'First the mixing stopped, then the costumes got smaller, and then the showgirl was taken out of the picture and replaced by nude dancers,' says Cathy Saxe forlornly, who outperformed 200 competitors to win her job as a Copa girl at the Sands. Now, she says 'the parading showgirl is a thing of the past.'

Not quite. In fact, showgirls have proven to be so popular that recently they've come back to other casinos as well. In 2001, Caesars Palace brought in sexy girls called 'shadow concierges' to perform choreographed routines behind a sheer screen. The same year, the MGM Grand established a permanent home for 13 original members of the French dance troupe, Crazy Horse. Crazy Horse in Paris is famous for its productions celebrating women and the artistry of the nude.

TROPICANA BIRDMAN

The Tropicana sports a kind of funky, old-fashioned charm; it promotes a Caribbean theme, with a flamingo-filled waterpark and a wildlife habitat whose colorful birds include macaws and toucans. Labyrinthine corridors lead from the flower garden to the casino, in whose Tropics Lounge is the 'Birdman,' otherwise known as animal trainer Joe Krathwohl. It's a free show (daily except Thursday) during which eagles and parrots perform such unlikely tricks as riding scooters, and being juggled by Krathwohl himself.

In summer, water-soaked gamblers can swim up to a blackjack table at the edge of the pool, doubtless using cards supplied by Kem Plastic Playing Cards Inc. of Scranton, Pennsylvania, whose cellulose-acetate decks survive constant rewashing. Plastic cards are especially favored by poker tables, because they hold up to the oils on the skin when they are heavily handled.

LEGENDS OF THE PAST

The Tropicana is fast cornering the market on nostalgia. One of the 'must-sees' is the fascinating **Casino Legends Hall of Fame**, tucked away behind a delicatessen, displaying items from hundreds of casinos, many of which are now defunct. Historical documents and photographs line the walls of this excellent gambling museum, which traces the past 70 years of Las Vegas through its vast collection.

The 15,000 or so items include colorful gambling chips, autographed boxing gloves, hotel security uniform patches, ancient slot machines and porcelain decanters shaped like slot machines, packets of Desert Inn cigarettes, record album covers and glittering, bespangled costumes worn by a variety of performers.

A videotape of various hotels (Aladdin, Hacienda, the Sands) being imploded runs continually, near to a glass case of memorabilia from El Rancho Vegas (1941–60) and a catalogue from

> **Tall tale**
> Chorus line personalities have to measure up in every possible way. Here are the Las Vegas minimum height requirements to be in a show on the Strip:
>
> • acrobats: 5 foot, 3 inches
> • dancers: 5 foot, 6 inches
> • showgirls: 5 foot, 10 inches

The Folies Bergeres came to the Tropicana in 1959

Map on page 20

the Sands' auction in July 1996. On another screen, a film displays the antics of the Sinatra-led 'Rat Pack'. There is an admission charge to the museum (open daily, 7am–9pm) but free tickets are often handed out – along with a free slot machine pull – in the hotel's parking lot.

Below: Sky Screamer, MGM
Bottom: making a
Grand entrance

THE MGM GRAND

Across Tropicana Avenue from the parking lot, a red traffic sign counts down the seconds allowed for crossing over to the fleet of gold limousines which sit outside the ★★★ **MGM Grand ❹**. Guests waiting to check in and out are handled at 38 reception-desk windows. They watch panoramic images of desert scenes, baseball stadiums and advertisements on an 80-panel video screen, to help allay the frustration of what is sometimes a lengthy wait. Opened in late 1993, the MGM Grand has enough rooms and suites to keep a dedicated guest going for almost 14 years if they wanted to stay in a different room every day. When the luxury high-roller suites (some containing 27 telephones) are rented to ordinary customers they cost $2,500 a night. Other rooms in the hotel are constantly being remodeled to enhance the comfort of their guests.

Its entrance is flanked by a 45-ft (14-meter) high lion, said to be the largest bronze statue in

the United States: the MGM Grand is huge in every way. (In an earlier version, visitors walked right through a giant lion to enter the casino, but it was replaced after somebody pointed out that in some cultures walking through a lion's mouth was not a lucky omen.) The air-conditioning system could cool a desert community of 5,500 homes. There are enough doors – 8,000 – to equip 1,600 three-bedroom homes, and one of the world's biggest casinos is the size of four football fields – 171,500 square ft (16,000 square meters).

On the casino floor, visitors walking through the glass entrance to the **Lion Habitat** may find lions sleeping over their heads. The beasts frolic with their trainer, Keith Evans, in a rocky enclosure with waterfalls. Three of the animals – Metro, Goldie and Louis B – are said to be descendants of the MGM signature lion whose yawn-like roar introduced the company's movies.

At the entrance on the Strip, a walkway from the Tropicana leads onto MGM's balcony over the casino floor. At the far side, live music or trailers from forthcoming movies are amplified on a giant screen.

To the left, in the amusing **Rainforest Cafe**, simulated thunderstorms and animated monkeys and crocodiles distract diners toying with dishes of food, amidst imitation birds, animals and gorgeous butterflies.

GRANDEUR AT THE GRAND

The hotel's 15 restaurants, some decorated with posters from old MGM movies, serve 30,000 meals a day. Fifty waiters and waitresses at a time handle room service, and though this is usually adequate, a Barbra Streisand concert will bring hundreds of high rollers (concert seats: $1,000) and thousands of breakfast orders. The rooms are cleaned by 740 maids working in dual-person teams, and 62 phone operators sing thousands of times a day the corporate mantra: 'Thank you for calling the MGM Grand, have a grand day.'

On their work days, employees get free cafeteria meals. All 6,000 employees wear uniforms

Star Attraction
● MGM Grand

Animal farm
Animal trainer Keith Evans drives into town every day with some of the 18 lions that he keeps at home on his estate outside Las Vegas, along with tigers, snow leopards and other beasts. At the MGM Grand, the lions are on show in a glass-enclosed African savannah-like enclosure located on one side of the casino.

A Knight to remember

Map on page 20

Keno
Even non-gamblers will have trouble escaping the clutches of keno. The game is everywhere: in bars, in coffee shops, in hotel lounges. Keno is, in effect, a lottery. The game uses 80 balls, numbered from 1 to 80. The house draws 20 balls at random, the results of which are displayed on an electronic board. If you guess the right numbers, you win. If you don't, you lose. What simpler way could there be to separate you from your money?

Neon delivery

devised to harmonize with the hotel's dominant hue of deep green. 'We wanted to maintain a dignified silhouette,' says Jackie Murphy, the costume and uniform manager.

Until now, all employees at Strip casinos – cocktail waiters, janitors, busboys, cooks, stagehands and others – have been required to get work cards or undergo police checks, but in 2001 the city contemplated making life a little easier for these low-level workers by eradicating these onerous and outdated laws.

NEON CRISIS

On the Strip, where even a decade ago there were 15,000 miles of neon tubing, the ongoing energy crisis has created problems. Bugsy Siegel placed a couple of 80-ft (24-meter) high neon champagne glasses outside the Flamingo in 1945, but by 1958 the Stardust's entire wall winked and blinked with Earth, comets, planets, and flaming meteors. Then came the era of taller and taller signs: the Dunes' 180-ft (55-meter) high sign in 1962; the Frontier's 220-ft (67-meter) high sign four years later. Finally, in 1984, Caesars Palace spent $1 million on its 32,000 bulb 'readerboard.'

Electronic, rather than neon, billboards are becoming more popular, writes a local expert, with neon regarded as 'the old Vegas.' But although these huge promotional devices consume a lot of megawatts, they are not something the casinos feel they can abandon. Hence, the area has suffered from the energy crisis the state has endured since the turn of the millennium.

NO ENERGY TO SPARE

Although the flashy look of the Strip will continue, the casinos are being forced to cut back in other ways, and some have added surcharges to the cost of hotel rooms. The typical Strip casino uses each day about the same amount of electricity as 10,000 homes, and casino bills have risen by as much as 46 percent. Thus, thermostats are going into unused convention rooms, and the amount of electricity used throughout the hotels is being reduced. Even the slot machines have not escaped scrutiny; according to the manufacturers, new ones will consume 25 percent less power.

MGM's casino is still the biggest in town, and significantly, has 3,500 slots, that is 1,000 more than its nearest rival.

Slot machine betting, the fastest growing game of the 1990s, increased another 12 percent recently. Casinos earn $1 billion a year just from nickel slots. MGM Mirage's patent on coinless slot machines (which use paper currency, coupons or 'cash-out' slips) has been licensed to Reno's International Game Technology (IGT), the world's largest manufacturer of slot machines, which has about 85 percent of the market.

FREE TV SCREENINGS

This bustling 'Crossroads of the World' is the perfect place – in the opinion of CBS television – to solicit opinions on its forthcoming shows. Outside the MGM Grand, about 600 visitors each day are stopped and invited to attend free screenings to give their opinions on pilots or prototypes for new series that the network is testing. In return they are offered $10 discount certificates that can be used in the adjoining Television City gift shop. The CBS executives

Below and bottom:
Strip shows

Map on page 20

Commercial possibilities
Commercials filmed in the state of Nevada in 1999 generated $16 million over the course of just 22 production days. In 2000, the overall revenue generated was $123 million, or 50 percent more than in the previous year. Great weather, willing 'extras' and easy proximity to Hollywood are some of the factors sited as to the state's popularity with the makers of ads.

find them a willing audience. 'People come here for the night life and try to figure out what to do during the day,' one commented. 'This is a place where people have time to spare.'

It is a 15-minute walk from the hotel entrance to what used to be the 33-acre (13-hectare) MGM Grand Adventures theme park, now renamed the **Park at the MGM Grand**. This amusement area is a much scaled-down version of its original self, and is now open only to private groups (from 50 to 7,000). The eventual fate of this land is widely speculated upon; rumors of a casino with a San Francisco theme dominate.

Behind the time-share Polo Club, a monorail curves around connecting the MGM Grand with Bally's casino. The long-time ambition of Las Vegas authorities is to connect Downtown, the Strip and McCarran airport; investors have come up with $600 million for the monorail to run from the MGM to the Sahara.

SPIELBERG'S GRAND CANYON

Adjoining MGM Grand is the **Showcase Mall**, recently themed as the **Grand Canyon**, with the aid of 60 tons of textured 'rock,' rope bridges and a hovering helicopter. Lightning storms and flash floods are features of the hourly show. Harness-equipped climbers ascend the studded

The Showcase Mall, recently themed as the Grand Canyon

concrete 'tree' and others take an elevator up the 100ft- (30-meter) high Coca Cola bottle.

Kids will love the mall's **GameWorks**, the video playground created by Steven Spielberg. A joint venture between DreamWorks, Sega Enterprises and Universal Studios, games run the gamut from old-time pinball machines to full-motion rides like Power Sleds, a Japanese-based game where several racers are pitted against each other on the same icy course. No need for cash either (not that many people have cash left after a couple of days in Vegas); patrons buy a Smart Card from which all rides, attractions, food and drink are debited.

Below: MGM Grand's former doorway
Bottom: kids love Las Vegas

HEAVEN IS A CHOCOLATE BAR

Chocolate is another theme of the Grand Canyon. Among the mall's stores is **Ethel M Chocolates**, named after Ethel Mars, who in 1911 began making and selling chocolates from her home; her son, Forrest Mars, Sr, turned the family business into the chocolate empire it is today. Mr Mars, now in his 90s, lives mostly in Miami, but for about two months of the year, he stays in a penthouse above the Nevada factory and watches through one-way mirrors the employees, who call him the 'phantom of the candy factory.' Forrest established the factory in Nevada 'because it is one of the few states that allowed the sale of liqueur-filled cordials.'

Tours of the factory, near the desert town of Henderson, can be taken *(see page 76)*.

Mars certainly has made its mark in the mall; witness the huge, four-story **M & M's World**. A favorite with younger kids (be sure to feed them before entering), M & M's follows the adventures of four chocolate buttons (Red, Blue, Yellow and Green) in a series of exhibits, the M & M Academy, and a 3-D movie featuring Yellow and Red's trip to Vegas.

Fans of the candy should stop by Colorworks on their way out, where every color of peanut and plain M & Ms are on sale – even the elusive silver and gold ones.

Map
on page
20

2: Egypt, King Arthur and the Beach

Luxor – Excalibur – Mandalay Bay

3800–3950 Las Vegas Boulevard (The Strip)

Vegas vignette
Around these parts, 'if something is worth doing, it's worth overdoing,' says local columnist John Smith.

The 30-story, glass-paneled ★★★**Luxor** ❺ pyramid, it is said, has an atrium big enough to hold nine Boeing 747s airplanes, and the beam of light from its summit shines 10 miles (16 km) into the sky, running up an electricity bill of $1 million a year. Green laser beams from the eyes of the 100-ft (30-meter) Sphinx beside the entrance can project a 55-ft-high (17-meter) hologram of King Tut's head onto a water screen, but the Federal Aviation Administration has asked for a moratorium on these lasers after complaints from airplane pilots.

Below: Luxor spa
Bottom: Tut Museum

HIEROGLYPHICS

Past the hieroglyphic-covered walls and through the glass doors with pyramid-styled handles, the visitor is confronted by simulated archaeological digs, talking camels, a trio of theaters with motion simulators presenting 'participatory adventures,' and a recreation of Tutankamen's tomb, with replicas of its contents when it was discovered in 1922. Even the Luxor's carpet motifs are lotus blossoms and palm fronds in 15 different patterns, all evoking ancient Egypt and all custom-woven in Britain in sturdy wool-nylon blends. Less-trafficked areas such as hotel corridors get less expensive printed nylon carpets.

Many of the Luxor's 4,404 guest rooms are accessed by elevators called inclinators that turn sideways and run horizontally along rollers at 39° when they reach the upper floors. You have to be a guest to ride the inclinators, but only the 27th floor hallway offers a view, down onto the fourth-floor with its simulated and sanitized Times Square-type complex. Here, in a thickly-carpeted area reached via elevators from the lobby, are video arcades, an **IMAX theater**, and video karaoke machines allowing you to make your own music video backed by a choice of 700 music tapes. The IMAX show, *Secrets of the Luxor Pyramid*, was created by *Back to the Future* designer Douglas Trumbull. In three parts, each lasting about half an hour, the film takes participants underground on an adventure of exploration, which includes a 3-D vision of a solar eclipse over Egypt, and a time trip.

The theatrical Blue Man Group, at the Luxor Theatre, presents a fusion of offbeat humor, tribal music and stunning visual effects, while *Imagine* is a journey through time, a theatrical odyssey of music and top-notch specialty acts.

Star Attraction
● The Luxor

DREAMS OF LUXURY

'The owners of Luxor,' wrote noted architectural writer Aaron Betsky, 'chose that name not only to promote an Egyptian theme but also because it conjured up dreams of luxury. Money is gambled away every single day by people who can barely afford to live in the glamorous world Las Vegas has invented.'

Naturally, the Luxor's gamblers are no more distracted from their true obsessions by the grand picture than those of any other casino. A Californian visitor won a $3.8 million jackpot on one of its Megabuck slot machines, and many of the slots incorporate 'bill validators' which accept currency of up to $100 bills. Most slot machines,

Below: Blue Man Group
Bottom: pyramid power

Map on page 20

Map on page 20

Time will tell
Casino designers work hard to blur the distinction between fantasy and reality, day and night, in order to keep customers on the premises, and gambling. Notable among these ploys is an absence of clocks. Anyone who needs to know the time should head straight for a casino's Sports Book, the area where horse races, football games and other sports events are televised. Because the timing of races is all-important to the placing of bets, there are clocks a-plenty to be found.

which theoretically cost a quarter or a dollar, only pay out substantial sums if two or three coins are deposited instead of one, but Strip casinos are increasingly introducing interactive gaming machines, which allow players to make a selection from 10 different games by directly touching the screen.

The Luxor's lavish **Sports Book** area has individual television monitors for each seat, making it easy to bet in comfort. Sports Books owe their origins to Bugsy Siegel's Trans-America Wire Service, which once had the monopoly on relaying all horse race information in the US after the information left the race track. No bookie could operate without this information, and so Siegel could charge pretty much whatever he liked. Today a state commission sets the rates.

THE EXCALIBUR

'Welcome to the medieval time of your life,' reads the sign as you alight from the Luxor monorail at the ★ **Excalibur** ❻, the white Disney-style castle with its moat and drawbridge. Covering 57 acres (23 hectares) and costing $290 million, it is a family place filled with heraldic motifs, plastic knights bearing battle-axes and Sir Galahad's Prime Rib House. Past what seems like miles of wide carpeted cottages and the couple posing for

The Excalibur

photographs with their heads in the stocks, comes the Sherwood Forest Cafe and then the casino itself. Few visitors look upwards to notice the colored glass windows and cornices decorated with what look like genuine statues.

JOUSTING AND MINSTRELS

Strolling minstrels entertain and costumed figures roam through the Renaissance faire. Puppets, mimes, magicians and jugglers perform free every day from 10am on the Court Jester's Stage at Medieval Village. Merlin's Magic Motion Machine lures visitors into hydraulically activated seats for a ride in a runaway train, and also an outer space demolition derby directed by Hollywood's George Lucas.

The Excalibur's dinner show 'King Arthur's Tournament of Kings' features jousting. (An attempt to diversify away from the medieval theme and bring in live wrestling was a failure; customers are clearly happy with the attractions as they are.) The buffet holds 1,400 diners, but as in most casinos there's always a waiting line.

Kitchen Table Poker (i.e. free educational poker games) is conducted every morning for half an hour, after which participants put up $10 in real money to check out their newfound skills.

Charles L. Silverman, a designer of casino interiors, notes that the customer base is no longer just the gambler. 'It is anyone who walks through our doors. If enough people come in, enough of them will gamble, so we are creating lavish palaces to attract them.'

Ironically, it was the lowbrow Circus Circus group that produced first the Luxor, then the Mandalay Bay, changing their name to the Mandalay Resorts Group. They also own the Excalibur and the Monte Carlo, along with all the land on this side of the Strip for about a mile. It's obvious that the Strip will continue to expand southwards; one thing that is expected to go up is the world's largest Ferris wheel, a 518-foot (158-meter) high behemoth with 35 observation booths that will take half an hour to complete its circuit.

Below and bottom: encounters at the Excalibur

Map on page 20

Mandalay Bay

★★★ **Mandalay Bay** ❼, a tropical-theme resort on a lagoon with its own rum distillery, is many people's favorite casino, especially if the visitor happens to come from a chilly climate. The attractions are obvious: a pool with a sandy beach swept by real waves for body surfing, and a mythical Caribbean/Far Eastern atmosphere that exudes sun, sex and total relaxation.

Curiously, and for no immediately obvious reason, there is also a 20-ft (6-meter) tall headless statue of the founder of the Russian Communist party, Vladimir Lenin. This reproduction stands outside the very capitalist Red Square Restaurant, where the cheapest item on the menu is the Chicken Kiev at around 20 bucks. As they say in Las Vegas: go figure.

Mandalay Bay comes third in casino size – after the MGM and the Bellagio – and is experimenting with tracking customers and awarding them points for betting, buying things, eating in its restaurants and attending its shows. Mandalay Bay's showroom is in a bid to offer something for everyone: there are state-of-the-art translations of all of its theatrical presentations, via personal headsets that give plot developments throughout the show in Spanish, German, Italian, Japanese and Mandarin.

Shark Reef, an open 90,000 sq ft (8,400-sq-meter) aquarium holding 2,000 marine animals, was installed after the hotel opened and has proved to be very popular. Over a million gallons (4 million liters) of water spread around ancient temples, statues, old stone stairways and a sunken ship are a haven for thousands of fish of all types and sizes.

The exhibit contains a dozen different shark varieties, ranging from an enormous nurse shark, which in its coral reef habitat sucks its prey out of holes in the rocks, to a baby Port Jackson shark only a few inches long. The exhibit points out that, despite their fearsome reputation, millions of sharks are killed every year for every human killed by a shark. A recent exhibit is Snakes & Dragons, the former being pythons, the latter fish.

Ascending Angels

Mandalay Bay's Aureole, a bigger clone of the New York City restaurant, seats around 400 diners. All eyes are aloft when someone orders wine which is then retrieved by one of the 'wine angels,' (acrobatic women in black track suits) who climb a huge tower to choose the selection from among 10,000 bottles.

Shark Reef, Mandalay Bay

3: Magic and Motoring

Aladdin – Desert Passage – Imperial Palace – Harrah's – Bally's – Paris Las Vegas – Flamingo Hilton – Caesars Palace – Casino Royale – Desert Inn – Venetian
3300–3700 Las Vegas Boulevard (The Strip)

Map on page 36

An illuminated, oversized model of Aladdin's famous magical lamp is now part of the fledgling Neon Museum Downtown, but a 17-story version of the ★ **Aladdin** ❽ resort and casino opened on the Strip in the year 2000, and quickly received a less than magical welcome. 'The paint has barely dried on this city's newest monument to gambling and already the death watch has started,' commented the *Los Angeles Times,* blaming such 'miscalculations' as the lack of a grand, sweeping entrance and the need to climb stairs to reach the 'underwhelming' doors.

Star Attraction
● Mandalay Bay

REFRESHINGLY DIFFERENT

Of course, as is so often the case in such matters, the verdict is a matter of opinion. The very thing some critics don't like – where the exterior portion of the casino abuts on the Strip – is actually occupied by a refreshingly different walkway, shielded from the sidewalk below by shrubbery. And Aladdin executives say that any

Below: the Aladdin
Bottom: Desert Passage

Map below

basic flaws will be corrected over time and soon forgotten. The 2,567-room resort sits on the site of its namesake (dramatically imploded in 1998), where Elvis Presley married his teen-age sweetheart Priscilla in 1967. The whole place is themed after the magic-infused tales of *The Arabian Nights*, with flying carpets, ebony horses and an 'Enchanted Garden' of lights.

DESERT PASSAGE

More enchanting than the casino itself, however, is the surrounding **Desert Passage**, an exotic complex of 135 opulent stores and restaurants. Beneath a flawless blue and white sky, tiled benches, immense pottery jars and the occasional wall fountain line the smooth cobbled hallways, which are navigated by bicycle rickshaws (generous tips expected) for those who don't feel up to the walk. Street merchants dressed in Moroccan attire ply their wares from stylish kiosks, and occasional wedding parties – accompanied by belly dancers and musicians – navigate the throngs. The Endangered Species chain has a store (clothes, glass and plaster animals, jewelry), its entrance guarded by life-size stone elephants.

As for the subject of magic, it is becoming one of Las Vegas's preoccupations. In addition to Lance Burton *(see page 20)*, who is less than

Tricky customers
The skills evinced by magicians are pretty much the same ones employed by casino cheats. 'They're magicians, too,' says the *Las Vegas Advisor*. 'They're expert at diverting attention while they pull off their scam. The quickness of the hand deceives the eye.'

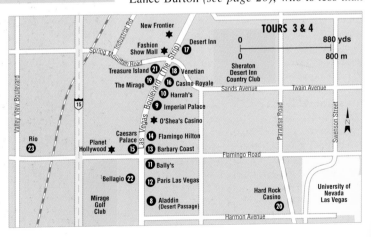

TOURS 3 & 4

halfway through a 13-year contract at the Monte Carlo casino, less well-known magicians perform throughout the city to a receptive audience. Some are giants such as Siegfried and Roy, who make lions and tigers disappear nightly in the Mirage showroom, or Steve Wyrick, with an eight-year contract at the Sahara, or locals Penn and Teller, who often pop up in the Rio's Samba Theatre.

The Hotel San Remo promotes the 'showgirls of magic,' a topless trio who perform sleight of hand in seductive, feathered costumes. And the Venetian bills belly-dancing Melinda as the 'first lady of magic' touting one of her tricks as the '100mph speeding car vanish.'

Las Vegas – where David Copperfield warehouses his enormous sets – has become the world's magic capital, not only because almost every magician aspires to play here, but because it can offer a certain stability for big shows. 'These are jaw-dropping spectacles that can't go on tour,' says MGM Mirage vice president, Alan Feldman, 'because they have to be presented in theaters designed for that purpose. Anyway, Las Vegas is in its own way an illusion where people come to escape, with a mind-set to be wowed.'

Below: London Club, Aladdin
Bottom: Imperial Palace

IMPERIAL PALACE

If you want to be wowed, then you could also visit the ★ **Imperial Palace ❾**. Owner Ralph Engelstad is Las Vegas' only sole proprietor of a major casino, and his $400-million fortune usually earns him a place in the *Forbes* 500 list of America's richest people. Opening in 1979 with an oriental theme, the Imperial Palace has a roof covered in blue tile from Japan. Inside are carved dragons, giant wind-chime chandeliers, and bars called Geisha, Ginza and Mai-Tai. Engelstad has been honored for his sympathetic approach to the disabled, who form 13 percent of his 2,600 employees.

The Imperial's twice-nightly *Legends in Concert* show, which has been running for 10 years, features impersonations of such performers as Liberace, Michael Jackson, Madonna and, of course, Elvis Presley.

Map on page 36

The show's creator, John Stuart, rotates his cast from about 100 impersonators who do shows in several countries, choosing from his five Marilyn Monroes and five Elvis Presleys.

Compulsive gambling
Harrah's is more upfront that many gaming companies about gambling addiction. The company's director of community relations says her company has been investing $250,000 a year in compulsive gambling programs. Harrah's is one of eight gaming companies represented on the Nevada Council of Problem Gambling, which aims to develop treatment resources, and displays large posters declaring 'Know when to Stop.' There's also a helpline number, tel: 1-800-522-4700.

ELVIS DROVE HERE

Owner Engelstad is renowned for his antique cars. The animated figure of John Wayne, standing beside his silver 1931 Bentley, welcomes you to the 200-car **Imperial Palace Auto Collection**; here you can admire an array of 1930s Duesenbergs, Liberace's 1981 Zimmer – whose hood ornament is the pianist's trademark candelabra – Howard Hughes's baby blue Chrysler, a 1929 Isotta Fraschini of the type seen in *Sunset Boulevard*, and a replica of Karl Benz's 1886 three-wheeler said to have reached speeds of 8 mph (13 kph), as well as cars once owned by Adolf Hitler, Nikita Khrushchev and most US presidents. The blue and white 1976 Cadillac, for which Elvis Presley paid $14,409 (including such extras as brass hubcaps) and Marilyn Monroe's 1955 coral pink Lincoln Capri convertible are also on display.

★ **Harrah's** ❿, which opened in the 1970s as an enormous Holiday Inn, replaced its famous riverboat facade with an exterior featuring gold-trimmed harlequins; it celebrated its $200 million new look by staging a high-wire walk 100 ft (30

Bally's showgirls

meters) above the Strip by circus great, Tino Wallenda. The company owns 18 other properties, including the Rio, west of the Strip.

Harrah's is an exuberant place. The Bally Pro Slot machines are advertised as having a 'noisy stainless steel tray so that payoffs are truly exciting.' The trays are designed to foil those who do not want to draw attention to their winnings – coin cups can't be placed in them to deaden the sound.

BALLY'S

On the corner to the south, ★ **Bally's** ⓫ has installed four 200-ft (60-meter) long people movers, surrounded by a cascading water feature, lighted pylons and giant palm trees. Every 20 minutes the entry area erupts with a sound-and-water show involving a wave machine and blow-hole fountains. Water seems to be something of a theme here. In a multi-million dollar show called *Jubilee*, the *Titanic* sinks on stage.

Bally's has doubled the size of its baccarat room to target the kind of gamblers who are willing to wager up to a million dollars on their Las Vegas trips. (The industry term for gamblers willing to wage hundreds of thousands of dollars on a single hand is 'whales.') Because of its liberal odds and high-bet limits, baccarat is a favorite with high rollers, and in one recent year, the Strip's 55 baccarat tables generated $594 million compared with the $482 million yielded by almost 900 blackjack tables. Collectively, of course, it's the slot machines that bring in the most money, but the competition is fierce.

A $25 million monorail links Bally's with the MGM Grand, the first local monorail system between separately owned gambling resorts and which, sometime in the future, is expected to be extended all the way to downtown Las Vegas. A further planned monorail will pass through the Bellagio, Caesars Palace and the Mirage.

After Bally's, another monorail stop is at the $800 million ★★★ **Paris Las Vegas** ⓬. Joined by Le Boulevard, a street of shops and French restaurants, both are owned by Park Place Entertain-

Star Attraction
● Paris Las Vegas

Below: Harrah's
Bottom: a player and
a gentleman

Map on page 36

Around the world in 80 casinos

ment, whose empire includes 16 other gaming properties throughout the US, and properties in Australia and Uruguay. Paris's most prominent landmark is the 50-story Eiffel Tower, rising 540 ft (165 meters), a half-size scale model of the original. Before it opened, the casino's publicity boasted that the French version would lower their lights in tribute to coincide with the Vegas opening, but nobody now seems sure whether it happened or whether the announcement was a typical piece of Vegas hype. Nice try, though.

The colossal legs of the tower are solidly planted in the 85,000-sq-ft (7,900-sq-meter) casino, which houses an attractive fountain, but also a plethora of signs, such as Le Salon des Tables, Les Toilettes, La Réception, Le Bell Captain and Les Artistes Steak House.

ROMANTIC REPLICAS OF PARIS

A romantic, lamplit bridge straddles the casino high above the room, but access is available only to those who have paid admission to climb the tower. There's a French restaurant at the top – one of eight at the casino – but you might prefer to linger and watch passing crowds from Mon Ami Gabi, a raised café just above the sidewalk.

Fronted at the Strip by the massive Academie National de Musique, Paris Las Vegas's other replicas include the Arc de Triomphe, the Champs Elysées, the Louvre, the Opera House and the Palace of Versailles. There are shops selling chic Parisian fashion and the casino has 2,200 slot machines in total.

Down the block, the **Barbary Coast** ⓭ sports chandeliers with big white globes, Art Deco glass signs and waitresses wearing red garters on black net stockings. Some tables are set aside for Pai Gow, a form of poker adapted from an Oriental domino game, and a poker machine played with gold coins pays $250,000 for a royal flush and offers a free drink for two pairs.

Its upscale neighbor, the ★ **Flamingo Hilton** ⓮, is heralded by life-size models of the birds flanking the entrance, and a tropical scene depicting more of them stretching for 50 ft (15 meters) behind the reception desk. The ballroom is studded with chandeliers containing 20,000 crystals from Spain, along with 35,000 ft (10,500 meters) of fiber-optic wiring which enables them to glow pink, red, green, yellow, blue and orange. Seven of the chandeliers are 20 ft (6 meters) high, and all were designed by French artist Claude Boeltz, who in his earlier days in France worked with Picasso and Dali.

BULLET-PROOF OFFICE

Memories of the Mob-run original Flamingo are evoked by Bugsy's Bar and Bugsy's Celebrity Theater. Siegel's bullet-proof office, with its elaborate escape routes, was demolished in 1995, and is commemorated by a plaque in the garden which states wryly that his 'preoccupation with safety proved to be geographically misplaced' (he was murdered in Beverly Hills).

Among the slot machines in the casino, as in most others, are some relatively new Elvis Presley slot machines, which play age-old recordings by the King if you bet in a certain way. The hotel's garden – with yet more plastic flamingos and some *real* penguins – can make for a charming evening stroll away from the glitz and neon hubbub of the Strip.

Slot machines

Slots have a history that is over 100 years old, dating from when Charles Frey invented the original three-reel, Liberty Bell slot machine in his San Francisco workshop in 1898. By the time Bugsy Siegal added slots to his Flamingo Hotel in the late 1940s, the machines were spreading across America. At first they were seen as a way to entertain the wives and girlfriends of high rollers, but soon slots were bringing in more revenue than table games.

Le Salon des Tables

CAESARS PALACE

Map on page 36

★★ **Caesars Palace ⓑ** dominates the western side of the street, with its 50-ft (15-meter) cypresses, statues and a row of elegant fountains that Evel Knievel tried to jump over on a motorcycle. Near the central people mover at Caesars is a rotunda that houses a miniature model of the city of Rome, as it may have appeared 2,000 years ago. The 4,000-seat showroom planned for construction in 2002 will, we're told, resemble the Coliseum. Singer Celine Dion has signed a $45 million contract to appear at this lavish extravaganza five times a week for three years.

Below and bottom: a funny thing happened on the way to the Forum

Much of the Carrara marble for the swimming pools and statues came from the same Italian quarries that supplied Michelangelo with the stone for his 18-ft (5.5-meter) masterpiece, *David*, a copy of which sits here between the hotel's two towers. Another of the statues is of Joe Louis, who worked for the hotel as a 'greeter'; it is both a tribute to the former heavyweight boxing champion and a reminder of the 100 major bouts that have been staged here. Caesars, always big on sports, was the first venue in Las Vegas to install satellite equipment to relay events to its Race and Sports Book. Caesars also specializes in fun-but-pricey 3-D motion simulator rides, of which the best is *The Race for Atlantis*, located in the **IMAX theater** off the magnificent Great Hall.

THE FORUM

The classy arcade known as the **Forum Shops** – Dior, Versace, Gucci, Bulgari, Ferragamo – is always crowded. Stores range from a clock shop called Roman Times to Warnerius Fraternius Studius Storius (Warner Bros Studio Store). A perpetually flying pig welcomes customers to Magnet Maximus. Here, a vaulted ceiling emulates a changing sky over the arches, columns, fountains and central piazza, where celebrity chef Wolfgang Puck's Spago's restaurant adjoins a replica of the Trevi Fountain.

At one end of the arcade, beneath a pale blue ceiling with puffy white clouds, is an enormous statue of Minerva. In another piazza, Bacchus sits on an elevated throne. Every now and again, the throne revolves, the god raises a beaker to his lips and speaks, as laser-driven planets and constellations race through the sky above. Plutus controls the music and dancing waters, and Apollo strums a modern fiber-optic lyre.

The curtains of a stage beside the lounge are closed, marked by a sign reading: 'Their empire is vast: its boundaries seemingly endless. Caesar and Cleopatra will return shortly.'

CASINO ROYALE

As you exit the Forum Shops at the Cyber Station end of Caesars, you can see the bright blue and violet windows of the **Casino Royale** ⑯, just across the Strip. However, you have to take the moving walkway all the way back through the casino to exit. Once inside the Casino Royale you can don a Victorian costume and be photographed against an appropriate background at Madame Bloomer's Old Time Photo.

Across the Strip, the venerable **Desert Inn** ⑰ – the only Strip hotel with its own golf course – looks even classier with a sweeping cream-colored façade. If you feel in need of haute cuisine, the Desert Inn houses Nevada's only AAA-rated Four Diamond restaurant, the Monte Carlo. The food is wonderful but pricey, and, unlike in other restaurants, patrons dress up for the occasion.

Star Attraction
● Caesars Palace

The sound of money
Casinos are still experimenting with 'coinless' slot machines, which use plastic or paper and require winnings to be traded in at the cashier's cage. These have not proved popular in the past, however, because customers complain about not being able to hear the distinctive clanking of the winners' coins.

Casino Royale

Map on page 36

Below: gondolas and the Doge's Palace

The Venetian

Viewed from the Strip, the ★★★ **Venetian** ⓭ is the most sensational of all the Las Vegas hotel-casinos, and is a true testament to the power of magic. It really *looks* like Venice (albeit a small, somewhat cramped Venice), from the Campanile Bell Tower ringing 300 ft (90 meters) above the Grand Canal to the *gondolieri* – some of whom were imported from Italy for the grand opening of the hotel – in striped shirts who serenade their sometimes-embarrassed passengers. Adding even more realism, thousands of pigeons have been trained to fly in and swirl around the place at least twice a day.

Built at a cost of $1.5 billion on the site of the former Sands Hotel, which was imploded without the usual Vegas hype, the Venetian was designed to be the world's largest hotel and convention complex under one roof, with enough marble and stone flooring to cover a dozen football fields. Sophia Loren cut the rope and smashed a $100 bottle of champagne on a gondola to mark the opening.

The rooms (average cost $167) are almost twice as large as those at most hotels; the restaurants are all manned by chefs on the critics' top 10 lists; the luxurious spa – the largest on the Strip – is operated by the renowned Canyon Ranch, leader in its field; the prestigious Guggenheim Museum in New York, in partnership with Russia's The Hermitage, operates the hotel's fine art **Guggenheim Museum**; and the convention center is almost as big as the one operated by the city. When the Venetian's second building phase is completed, it will also have hundreds more rooms than any of its rivals (6,000).

In addition to the Doges' Palace and Rialto Bridge (where the moving sidewalk leads, improbably, to the British-originated Madame Tussaud's), the resort contains Piazza San Marco, in which jugglers, singers and dancers always seem to be performing. The square is the culmination of the **Grand Canal Shoppes**, which begins with an awe-inspiring frescoed ceiling and segues into the bluest skies ever seen.

4: Merely Spectacular

The Mirage – Hard Rock Casino – Treasure Island – the Bellagio – the Rio
3400–3600 Las Vegas Boulevard (The Strip)

In a city of hotel-casinos constantly outdoing each other, the merely spectacular has become almost commonplace. Until a year or two ago, the resorts dreamed up by Steve Wynn –the Mirage, Treasure Island and the Bellagio – were the most stupendous venues on the Strip. He sold the trio to MGM Mirage, and they're still unimaginably spectacular to anybody who's not used to this sort of thing, but Vegas being Vegas, the gasps these days are always over the newest place to open.

WYNN'S WINNERS

Of course, Steve Wynn is not the sort of fellow to be outdone by anybody, so when he sold his famous trio, it wasn't long before he announced plans for another new resort with which he clearly plans to up the stakes once more. It will probably cost $2 billion and will occupy the site of the Desert Inn, which he has bought with the sole aim of pulling down. Hollywood director Steven Spielberg is collaborating, and stunt rider Robbie Knievel is said to be planning to ride off the top of the hotel as it is imploded.

Map on page 36

Star Attraction
● The Venetian

Vegas vignette
'Las Vegas is what God would have done if he'd had the money.'
— Casino entrepreneur Steve Wynn

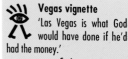

Hamburgers and hogs

Map
on page
36

Wynn is probably the best-known person in Las Vegas; after his jokey commercials with Frank Sinatra on TV a few years ago, his face became familiar to millions of Americans. Like most visionaries, he has made as many enemies as friends, and successfully sued publisher Lyle Stuart to bar further distribution of an unauthorized biography (*Running Scared* by John L Smith, Barricade Books, 1995), which accused him of everything from megalomania to mob connections. For some years he was America's highest paid executive.

Below: lion tamers
Bottom: Siegfried & Roy
with Cher

SUCCESS STORY

The son of a compulsive gambler who operated a bingo operation in Maryland, Wynn arrived in Las Vegas aged 25, invested $45,000 for a 3 percent interest in the Frontier Hotel and became its slots manager. It turned out that several stockholders were stand-ins for Detroit mobsters, and so Wynn was forced to sell early. However, he was befriended by the town's top banker, E. Parry Thomas, and with Thomas's help bought a liquor distributorship. He bought the first piece of Vegas property that Howard Hughes ever sold, a lot adjoining Caesars Palace, turning a quick profit of $766,000 when a nervous Caesars decided to buy the land rather than have him build.

Kenneth Feld, owner of Ringling Brothers Barnum and Bailey Circus, is a fan: '[Wynn] may call this the hotel business,' Feld says, 'but he's in the entertainment business, and he stands up there with [Disney's] Michael Eisner and Steve Spielberg for their combination of vision and their ability to make it happen.' Wynn *may* be up there on ability, but he far surpasses them in cash flow.

THE MIRAGE

Next on Wynn's schedule came gold-and-white, Polynesian-style ★★ **the Mirage ⓲**, which three years after its opening was the biggest money maker on the Strip. The Mirage needs more than a million dollars a day to break even, but it doesn't rely entirely on gambling. Its premier attraction – magicians and white tigers in the **Siegfried & Roy Show** – fills its 1,500 seat show room 480 times a year, despite tickets that are among the most expensive in town. The **Secret Garden of Siegfried & Roy** (admission fee) displays more wild animals amidst semi-tropical splendor. Past azure blue pools in which dolphins swim are several animals that have become extinct in the wild, largely because of poachers, but have been successfully bred in captivity.

Visitors are handed recording sticks over which messages from Siegfried and Roy can be heard. The messages are usually pretty bland and the animals are often asleep, but outside one sanctuary, Roy recounts on tape the occasion when he bit on the nose of a tiger which had pinned him down. He then made a 'friendship sound,' he related, 'and the tiger pretended it had never happened and jumped up.'

Down the sides of the Mirage, a volcano rushes 128,000 recirculated gallons (485,000 liters) of water a minute, and the eruptions are fed by a natural-gas pipeline 8 inches (20 cm) across. To mask the sulfuric odor of the burning gas, a pina colada scent was added. 'Steve (Wynn)'s first reaction to the volcano was concern that it would look like a cigarette lighter going off,' says designer David Hersey. 'I tried to assure him that it would look

Star Attraction
● **The Mirage**

> **A chip off the old block**
> Only a handful of security-conscious companies manufacture gambling chips, which, in Vegas, are as good as money. Casino officials are trained to check chips for an alpha-dot no bigger than a speck of pepper, an anti-counterfeiting device which, under magnification, yields encoded symbols. Three dimensional or holographic chips are also difficult to replicate, and popular with casino owners.

Atrium at the Mirage

Map on page 36

Poker pointers

A frequent tournament player, British writer A Alvarez, says: 'Poker is a game of many skills. You need card sense, psychological insight, a good memory, controlled aggression, enough mathematical know-how to work out the odds as each hand develops, and what poker players call a leather ass – patience. Above all, you need the arcane skill called money management, the ability to control your bankroll and understand the long-term implications of each bet so that you don't go broke during a session.'

In the swim

better than that.' Wynn had demanded that the water be white like Niagara Falls, so a hinged panel was built into the waterfall. 'We found out how far we had to pull the panel out to get the water to be white.'

When the Mirage opened in 1989, Wynn declared that there had been 'a terrible sameness' to earlier casinos. 'The public couldn't differentiate between the Sands, the Dunes, Aladdin and the Sahara. I wanted to take it to a new level. We presented this place as an alternative for people. I always knew others would follow, as they have, but it has happened much faster than even I expected.'

SCUBA EQUIPMENT

Plumbers at the Mirage don scuba equipment to maintain the waterfalls, while 17 florists work shifts around the clock pampering the foliage. David Hersey, who has won seven Tony Awards – some of which were for *Cats*, *Evita*, *Starlight Express*, *Les Misérables* and *Miss Saigon* – came from London to illuminate the hotel in incandescent gold because, he says, the Strip's existing displays of neon couldn't be topped.

The displays, along with the banana trees, 60-ft high (18-meter) palms, orchids and exotic animals, have obviously contributed to making the Mirage one of Nevada's biggest tourist attractions. With sharks swimming in a 20,000-gallon (75,000-liter) tank behind the registration desk, and dolphins and more white tigers in glass cases in the shopping arcade, the hotel's 3,044 elegant rooms are invariably 95 percent filled (the national average is 65 percent).

Mirage guests spend more than $700,000 a day on non-gambling pursuits. The revenue from the casino is what makes all the other extravagances possible. Only l00,000 sq ft (9,000 sq meters) of the Mirage's 4 million sq ft (372,000 sq meters) are devoted to gaming, but it's what brings in the big bucks.

The $20 billion collected in an average year by the nationwide casino business (about $9 billion of which comes from Nevada casinos, 70 of them in Las Vegas) surpasses the record industry income by 50 percent. It is triple that collected by the theme-park business and quadruple the amount generated by the movie industry. The name of the game, of course, is bringing in the gamblers, and some of the people who do it, such as Steve Cyr, have become legends.

HARD ROCK CASINO

Cyr, the subject of a recent magazine profile, specializes in enticing 'whales' – the industry term for high-rollers – to the ★ **Hard Rock Casino** [20], by applying what the magazine called 'a mixture of genial charm and rocket-fueled salesmanship.' He claims to look after 70 men who regularly gamble more than $100,000 per trip. 'My goal,' he says, 'is that a guy loses a hundred grand, shakes my hand and says, 'Steve, I had a great time; I'll see you next month.''

Needless to say, Steve Wynn takes a different tack and claims: 'We build places for folks who don't think of themselves as gamblers.' He says that a lot of gambling today is encouraged by the federal government. 'The states pummel citizens with the benefits of the easy dollar in gaming, which is not the right thing to say, because it's not that way. But the states did it.'

Below: mega-watt guitar
Bottom: Vegas's volcano

Map on page 36

The Bellagio and the Mirage were listed at first and second places in a *Business Week* story about casino income, and while the magazine didn't give figures for those casinos, it did reveal that even in fourth place, the Venetian generates more than $2,600 per sq foot or $27,800 per sq meter per day (the Venetian's casino occupies 116,000 sq ft/10,780 sq meters; the Bellagio's around 155,000 sq ft/14,400 sq meters).

Below: Cirque du Soleil
Bottom: Treasure Island

Like other casinos, the Mirage and two or three other casinos are noting an explosive growth in video poker, which previously had been more popular among locals than the reel-machines, (which accounted for as many as three quarters of the machines on the Strip). International Game Technology supplies 70–80 percent of the slots in use in US casinos. And new games are constantly appearing and being tested.

TREASURE ISLAND

At least as interesting as the Mirage is the neighboring ★★ **Treasure Island** ㉑, which shares the 100-acre (40-hectare) site and is connected by a free tram. As you exit the tram you might be greeted with clapping and applause from all the folk waiting to board it. Treasure Island's showroom hosts the town's perennially popular attraction, **Cirque du Soleil** (one of two full-time

Cirque du Soleil shows playing everyday along the Strip), with 1,500 seats selling for good prices. And the sidewalk outside is the scene of a spectacular sea battle in which two full-sized ships wage war with each other in a vast man-made lagoon several times a day (starting in the late afternoon and going on till nearly midnight seven days a week).

A pirate ship, the *Hispaniola*, sinks the British frigate *HMS Britannia* after numerous fiery explosions. This spectacle predictably causes traffic jams and virtually halts pedestrian traffic on the Strip every time it happens. The show has a cast of 30 stuntmen and actors. Performances are at 4pm, 5.30pm, 7pm, 8.30pm and 10pm, with an extra 11.30pm show on Friday and Saturday.

PIRATE VILLAGE

Designers Jon Jerde and Roger Thomas scoured the world to find the shutters, window grilles, cannons and cauldrons that were replicated for Treasure Island's 18th-century **pirate village**. Then they borrowed craftsmen and designers from Hollywood. They said they were delighted to create something that wouldn't be destroyed when the film ended.

Treasure Island's horticulturists need to be taught rappelling and climbing so they can reach plants in the nooks and crannies of the pirate village's waterfront. The casino has waitresses in skimpy pirate costumes and croupiers clad in brocaded vests. Overhead are treasure chests overflowing with fake jewelry.

Some slot machines are labeled Swashbucklers, and the Treasure Island Store sells stuffed parrots as well as 8oz (227g) boxes of individually wrapped truffles. (Both the Mirage and Treasure Island have a deal with the Seattle Chocolate Company, which makes similar boxes for the Bellagio bearing pictures of the namesake Lake Como town.) There's a toy shop called – as you would expect – Captain Kids.

Mutiny Bay is an amusement center with mostly video games, and at the entrance are two

Star Attraction
● Treasure Island

Token of faith
Today's big spenders can find slot machines that accept $500 tokens for just one pop at the game.

Below and bottom: Las Vegas plays host to big chiefs

Map on page 36

animated skeletons in pirate costume who cackle and wave their bony arms. Inside the casino is a 13th-century column of carved limestone from Morocco, and eight fiberglass copies of the columns stand in Captain Morgan's Lounge. The aluminum chandeliers are made from bone molds taken from skeletons.

Weldon Simpson, designer of the Excalibur, the Luxor and the MGM Grand, says 'Las Vegas is better than virtual reality because in virtual reality you have to trick your mind into thinking that you are someplace else – many other places.' Eventually, he believes, slot players will be enclosed in a private virtual-reality environment allowing 3-D interaction in a game based on the hotel theme. The more the gambler plays, the further he advances in the virtual reality game. 'It will be like playing Nintendo. When you get enough points you will become one of the virtual reality characters yourself.'

For all those people who are suffering from sore feet, a recent 200-ft-long (60-meter) bridge now crosses the Strip to connect Treasure Island with the Venetian, meaning you no longer have to walk miles to cross the street here.

Via Bellagio

THE BELLAGIO

Wynn's spectacular casino, the ★★★ **Bellagio ㉒**, is now owned by MGM Mirage, headed by Kirk Kerkorian, the world's biggest gambling operator, under whose purview are the Bellagio, Treasure Island, New York-New York, the Golden Nugget and golfing's exclusive Shadow Creek, as well as properties in the Nevada desert.

Kerkorian, a former high school dropout now aged 80 plus, paid Steve Wynn $6.7 billion for his resorts. 'He doesn't do it for the money, he has more money than he'll need in five lifetimes,' says a friend of KK's. 'He does it because he gets bug-eyed like a little kid when he goes through the place.'

Even to people who had become accustomed to the luxury of all the new casinos, the advent of the Bellagio caused gasps of admiration. It is said to have cost $1.6 billion to build and needs a further $2.5 million a day to make it pay for itself. It has almost 9,000 employees.

WATER, WATER EVERYWHERE

Water, that most precious of desert commodities, is the Bellagio's theme. Crossing the bridge from Bally's across the Strip, visitors hear opera booming out over a 8.5 acre (3-hectare) lake, on which hundreds of fountains dance to music perfectly programmed to coordinate with jets as high as 240 ft (73 meters), fading away into clouds of mist for the quieter interludes.

Guests registered with the hotel can tune into a special channel on their television sets to hear music synchronized with the water dance, and many of the rooms are located high enough so that the fountains spurt at eye level. The water comes from a tainted aquifer, via the resort's own treatment plant, to fill the lagoons in front of the Mirage and Treasure Island; the lake is meant to evoke Lake Como, the water on which the Bellagio's namesake village in Italy is located.

Long before the advent of the Venetian, Steve Wynn was thinking along similar lines with his (unfulfilled) vision of turning Downtown's Fremont Street into a canal – flooding two streets to create a Venice-like environment. Man-made

Star Attraction
● The Bellagio

The story of O
Cirque du Soleil's show at the Bellagio, 'O' (as in H_2O – water) is perhaps the most spectacular on the Strip, and seats are sold out weeks in advance. A melange of synchronized swimming, acrobatics, and theatrical effects, 'O' takes place in a specially designed theater that could never be replicated elsewhere. Tickets are expensive, but the show is unmissable.

Music is played to the Bellagio's water display

Map on page 36

lakes are theoretically banned in Clark County, but Wynn has political muscle. Shelley Berkeley, a University of Nevada regent, says: 'The Wynns are probably the most potent political force in the state of Nevada at this time.'

Plants and flowers are distributed lavishly around the Bellagio, nowhere more so than just beyond the lobby in a delightful conservatory with a 50-ft-high (15-meter) glass ceiling, and a botanical garden which changes with the seasons. The hotel employs 150 people on its gardening and greenhouse staff alone.

GRAND MASTERS

Below: Le Cirque
Bottom: Bellagio's gardens change with the seasons

Off to one side, a pianist plays at the Petrossian café, one of 17 different eating places. Star restaurants here are the offshoot of New York's famous **Le Cirque**, as well as the **Picasso**, with its furniture and carpet designed by Claude Picasso, son of the painter. Some of the master's pictures hang on the walls. Art, of course, gets a lot of attention at the **Bellagio Gallery of Fine Art**, which opened with great fanfare and a world-class collection, including paintings by Renoir, Monet, Van Gogh, Rembrandt and Picasso.

The gallery, which charges a stiff admission fee even to hotel guests, was another inspiration by Wynn, who bought three of its pictures for his per-

sonal collection when he sold the Bellagio. All throughout one summer, the gallery exhibited the collection of movie star and Oscar presenter Steve Martin, who counts works by Roy Lichtenstein, Picasso and Hockney among his possessions.

After the MGM Grand, the Bellagio is the largest casino in Vegas, but it is of a different quality. It may not rival Monte Carlo (the real one, in Europe), but *The Wine Spectator* rated the Bellagio's gaming room as 'positively demure, the kind of place where a gent can feel comfortable in a dinner jacket.'

HIGH ROLLERS

The Bellagio has a street of beautifully-designed shops whose stars – most foreign designers – include Armani, Prada, Chanel, Tiffany, Gucci and Hermès. The hotel's **Shadow Creek golf course**, lined with 21,000 pine trees from California and Arizona, is frequented by high rollers who can afford the $500 greens fee. This does include limousine transportation to and from the links, however, as well as a golf cart and the services of a caddy. Lord knows what kind of tip the caddy usually receives.

Tipping is a serious matter in Las Vegas, where croupiers have occasionally been known to retire from gratuities from overly generous winners. As a rule, though, they rely on tips to supplement their minimum wage scale, and if you're on a lucky streak it's quite okay to place a bet for the dealer as well as yourself.

Bartenders, cocktail waitresses, small-change ladies and casino personnel in general, as well as pool attendants, waiters, showroom guides and maitre d's all expect a reasonable gratuity to keep things moving smoothly. And if you've been a lucky winner at the end of your stay, don't forget the underpaid maid who cleans your room every day.

Despite the hotel's grandeur, some of the Bellagio's swimming pools in the back of the hotel – which are enhanced with Italianate fountains and 'mist showers' that spray the air every few

Nevada-style action
TV ads for a recent Las Vegas high roller fantasy sweepstakes had to be toned down when two of the networks objected to the term 'high roller.' They claimed it promoted gambling. The slightly modified ads did run, but even these were a huge step forward. A decade ago, says creative director Randy Snow, even the word 'casino' was banned. 'We used to refer to it as 'Nevada-style action.''

Nevada is known for its golf courses

Map on page 58

Taking a break from the gaming tables

minutes to provide a cooling breeze – failed to make the cut in the evaluations of Strip pools by *Where Las Vegas*. The magazine gave top marks instead to the famed waves on Mandalay Bay's sandy beach. *Where* also applauded Caesars Palace's Garden of the Gods, which claims inspiration from Rome's Baths of Caracalla. The Bellagio should take note.

THE RIO

At the ★ **Rio** ㉓ All-Suite Casino Resort, you can get what is probably the best eating deal in town, at the Carnival World Buffet in the Ipanema Tower. Eleven food counters include Chinese, Japanese, Mexican, fish & chips, salads, fruit and pastries, as well as the Village Seafood Buffet in the Masquerade Tower. If your stomach can cope with the indigestion potential of the bargain, you can have a dozen meals for the single price of around six bucks for breakfast (any time after midnight), to 13 bucks for dinner.

The Rio is very good on food and drink. The **Napa**, a French restaurant, whose chef Jean-Louis Palladin was chef at Washington, DC's Watergate, was nominated by *Gourmet* magazine as the best in town, while the **Wine Cellar Tasting Room** claims to have the world's largest stash of fine and rare wines – a $10 million collection – with hundreds of them available by the glass.

The **Rio Club** features late-night live entertainment and dancing. Guests are also allowed to use the **Rio Secco Golf Club**, which is located 15 miles (24 km) from the resort.

SHOW IN THE SKY

Several times every day except Tuesday and Wednesday, the Rio's **Masquerade Village** stages a 12-minute sequence called *Show in the Sky*. This is where guests don exotic costumes and ride above the audience in floats and gondolas. Take a look at the sandy beach and waterfalls beside the tropical lagoon, and try to catch the panoramic view from the hotel's 51st floor.

5: Food, Film and Fun

Fashion Show Mall – New Frontier – Stardust – Circus Circus – Slots-A-Fun – Riviera – Sahara – Las Vegas Hilton
2500–3500 Las Vegas Boulevard (The Strip)

Few visitors come to Las Vegas solely to shop, but most of them do partake of some form of 'retail therapy' while in town. Despite the spate of new malls, the longtime **Fashion Show Mall** across the way from Treasure Island is still doing steady business. Big names such as Saks Fifth Avenue, Neimann-Marcus and Macy's will soon be joined by Nordstrom. The *Review Journal* quoted Peter Nordstrom as saying his Seattle-based chain had been thinking about Vegas for more than a decade. When all expansion is completed in 2003, the Fashion Show Mall will house more than 300 shops. In order to give the shopping center a more distinct identity on the Strip, there will also be a huge, 700-foot (213-meter) long cloud suspended over the entrance. Currently, the Mall's relatively uncrowded Food Court is blessedly free of slot machines.

Below: stop and shop here
Bottom: royal flush at the Rio

After years of troubled union strife, the venerable **New Frontier** ㉔ casino resumed normal operation but is still a prime candidate for being pulled down one of these days. For a while, the new San Francisco-themed casino was

Map
below

destined for this site, but there have been arguments about the actual ownership of this concept. Meanwhile, the scaled-down version of Micky Gilly's clone of his now-defunct Texas nightclub, complete with mechanical bull, packs in the crowds every evening.

THE STARDUST

The Stardust date from the 1930s

★ **The Stardust ㉕** – originally founded by Tony Cornero, who was famous for running gambling ships off the California coast in the 1930s – was later sold to alleged Cleveland mobster Moe Dalitz, who became a generous local benefactor and the recipient of testimonial dinners attended by important state officials. Purple predominates here in the baize of the gaming tables, the pattern of the carpets and the color of the chairs. Other early casinos made liberal use of red and black, perceived as passionate colors.

These days, however, the mystery has been taken out of gambling, so 'our casinos can be lighter, brighter and friendlier,' says Charles L Silverman, who has been designing casino interiors for 32 years. The Stardust exterior is bathed in lines of purple light, and colored mini fountains beside the entrance shoot jets into each other.

Says Aaron Betsky: 'On The Strip you are part of an elaborate urban theater. After four decades

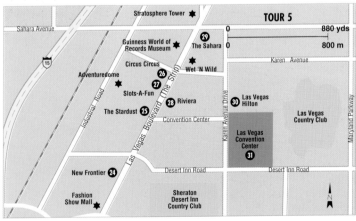

of trying, Las Vegas has finally managed to turn Hollywood into reality, and what we can learn from today's Vegas is that streets can also be theaters, buildings can become their own signs.'

Wayne Newton, listed in 1983 by *The Guinness Book of World Records* as the world's highest-paid entertainer, with earnings of around $325,000 weekly, used to play the Hilton, but is now fulfilling a lifetime engagement at The Stardust. He owns Casa de Shenandoah, a $7-million mansion on 52 acres (21 hectares) located about five miles east of the Strip on Sunset Road.

Newton has a tendency to take on the audience first-hand by leaping around the semi-circular runway to shake dozens of hands, then scores, then *hundreds* of hands. He reaches over people to make contact, runs up and down the aisles, kisses women young and old, smiles at everyone, waves to everybody he can't reach. At first this seems hilarious, then endearing. Many fans, who clearly idolize him, go home to Nebraska, to Idaho, or to Indiana and tell their friends, 'Wayne Newton shook my hand,' or 'Wayne Newton kissed me.' And so the legend grows.

CIRCUS CIRCUS

The Mandalay Resorts Group operates five major properties on the Strip, including the Luxor, Monte Carlo and Excalibur. In addition to the super-deluxe Mandalay Bay, the group also owns ★ **Circus Circus** ㉖, which is probably the most aggressively successful down-market, family-oriented casino in Las Vegas. Every day, for over 20 years, it has packed in the crowds with free circus acts, along with a midway lined with carnival concessions, lots of inexpensive food, a vast family amusement park and 5,100 parking spaces including an RV park. Some of the slots at Circus Circus are mounted on revolving platforms.

Preoccupied with their betting, Circus Circus gamblers rarely look up to where, overhead, a different world is populated by crowds jamming the midway attractions, as acrobats, jugglers, aerialists and clowns perform from 11am until

Gamblers' choice
The Nevada Gaming Commission recently allowed drug and grocery stores to install slot machines if they walled them off from the rest of the store. The directive banned slots specifically from the following: new liquor stores, gas stations, no-booze restaurants, car dealerships, motels, car washes and sandwich shops. Existing facilities are allowed to keep theirs.

Map
on page
58

Slots-a-fact

The popularity of slot machines has almost doubled since the 1970s, and they now typically account for 62 percent of a casino's winnings. The stakes are growing higher, too. 'Most casinos are getting on the slot band wagon,' says one expert. 'They recognize that it's the most stable customer base. It's people who are not trying to win big. They'll be back if they have fun.'

Below: coupon book
Bottom: the late Liberace

midnight. Miniature camels race along plastic tracks, children's faces are painted by a yellow-haired clown, and an endless line of hopefuls try to win prizes by bringing a huge mallet down heavily enough to propel a rubber chicken into a cooking pot.

Behind the casino, under an air-conditioned dome with palm trees, fake rock walls and life-size animated dinosaurs that roar, is the Adventuredome Theme Park. Experience the River Rapids on a double loop, double corkscrew roller coaster called the Canyon Blaster – and the Plunge, shooting over a 50-ft (15-meter) waterfall on a flume ride, passing tunnels, grottos, caves and 140-ft (40-meter) sandstone cliffs.

SLOTS-A-FUN

Next door is **Slots-A-Fun 27**, which offers free beer to all players and has penny slot machines – as they take only dollar bills, you get to play 100 pennies at a time. There's a glass case near the door exhibiting Polaroid photos of earlier winners, many of whom have taken advantage of the 'free pull' offered to customers who pick up one of the free ticket booklets.

Such satellite casinos are heavy on slot machines, which have become by far the biggest money-making sector in the gaming industry. The old one-armed bandits are becoming historical relics as they are replaced by electronic machines with TV screens instead of reels. Some slot machines accept special casino-issued credit cards, and almost all operate on multiple coins. Sometimes a number of progressive machines feed into one jackpot, where any machine in the group can win, and the jackpot grows into an astronomical amount of money.

These groupings can be a number of machines in one casino, or for traveling gamblers, can be tied to the same type of machine found throughout the state of Nevada. Progressive machines can be identified by flashing electronic payoff signs that are displayed either on top of the machine or above a grouping of machines.

THE RIVIERA

If you're more interested in feeding your stomach than the slot machines, one of the most convenient places to eat cheaply is at the 2,075-suite **Riviera 28**, at whose southern end is a fast-food court offering hot dogs, yogurt, burgers, Chinese, sushi, pizza, espresso and pastries. The Riviera, used for filming Martin Scorsese's 1994 film *Casino*, has a venerable entertainment history, having opened (in April 1955) with Liberace as its headliner. At a time when a home could be bought for $10,000, the pianist's $50,000 a week caused even more stir than having Joan Crawford host the show. In the 1950s, Orson Welles, Ginger Rogers, and Marlene Dietrich all played the Riviera; in the 1960s, Louis Armstrong, Tony Bennett and Sarah Vaughan followed.

Below and bottom: Casino was filmed at the Riviera

Today a 20,000-gallon (75,000-liter) aquarium is the venue for a variety show; drag artistes perform *An Evening at La Cage*; and the latest version of a rather tawdry skin show called Crazy Girls (which opened in 1987) begins with the audience being mooned by eight pairs of bare buttocks. (Seven Crazy Girls in bronze, their rears shiny from being caressed by thousands of hands, flank the casino's sidewalk entrance.)

Today's best state-of-the art slots can be found at ★ **The Sahara 29**. The slots are controlled by microchips which constantly generate a series

Map on page 58

Below: the King, plus kid

of random numbers, whether the machine is being played or not. Only the split second at which you pull the handle determines which numbers show up, your action merely telling the machine to inform you what has been already decided. Another gimmick is a video machine in which a pair of phantom hands appear to 'deal' the cards.

CYBER SPEEDWAY

A few years ago, the Sahara added a dramatic, neon-lit rotunda and a motif of neon camels. It also has an extensive **NASCAR Cyber Speedway** at the rear, where visitors can choose a type of car and course, then go on a virtual reality adventure; the life-size racing cars shake and sway up and down and side to side as a fast-moving racetrack is projected on an enveloping screen. This game imitates the **Las Vegas Motor Speedway**, a real-life track located outside town at 6915 Speedway Boulevard, which hosts races attended by luminaries from both racing and Hollywood.

The **Carroll Shelby Museum,** located on the same grounds as the motor speedway (tel: 702/643-3000, weekdays 8am–5pm) displays a range of performance cars.

The **Convention Center Hotel**, on Convention Center Drive, has 200 rooms and a swimming pool, but no casino or restaurants. This hotel used to be the Debbie Reynolds Hollywood Movie Museum until Miss Reynolds sold it to the World Wrestling Foundation, who by now have probably found another buyer.

Lots of high rollers do nicely at the **Las Vegas Hilton ❸⓿**. The hotel's opulent penthouse apartments, with their marble floors, chandeliers, fireplaces, gold-plated bathroom fixtures, individual pools, 24-hour butler and room service, workout facilities and media center, are turned over free to players spending in excess of $2 million. Elvis starred in more than 800 shows here.

Near both the Convention Center Hotel and the Hilton is the **Las Vegas Convention Center ❸❶**, a busy place once officials decided to aggressively pursue the lucrative trade convention market.

6: Downtown

Holy Cow – Stratosphere Tower – Fremont Street Experience – The Golden Nugget – Binion's Horseshoe – Four Queens – Lady Luck – Main Street Station

Heading north along the Strip towards Downtown, the **Holy Cow ㉜** Casino and Brewery displays above its entrance a life-sized, black and white, fiber-glass cow weighing 800 lb (360 kg). Cows are everywhere in the casino – painted on the ceiling and on the 'moo-la' slot machines. Visitors can shop in the 'cow shed' for cow hats, cow coffee mugs and cow T-shirts. They can also take free tours of the brew house, which makes 1,300 US gallons (5,000 liters) of beer every week. The plaza across the street is dominated by what boasts to be 'the world's largest souvenir shop.'

STRATOSPHERE TOWER

Here, near Sahara Avenue, is a colossal Las Vegas landmark, the ★★★ **Stratosphere Tower ㉝**. At 1,149 ft (350 meters), it is the tallest building in the American West and the tallest free-standing observation tower in the country. Speedy elevators whisk visitors to the finest views in Las Vegas in an ear-popping 30 seconds.

The tower, topped by observation decks and

Map on page 64

Star Attraction
● **Stratosphere Tower**

Below and bottom: the Stratosphere tower and view

Map
below

Big shots ride here

a revolving restaurant *(see page 95)*, offers thrilling rides hundreds of feet above ground, with its roller coaster and **Big Shot ride** – a kind of reversed bungee jump that shoots riders high into the air. There's a showroom, a pool and spa, and the choice of eating places includes the Around the World buffet and a 1950s diner.

Romantically inclined visitors can get married near the top of the tower which, needless to say, offers tremendous views.

CHEAP MOTELS

Between the Stratosphere Tower and Downtown proper there is not much of consequence beyond the occasional modest-sized gaming hall (more favored by locals than tourists) and the least expensive motels.

Often there is no particular advantage in seeking out a cheap motel, because a classier room can be found for the same price at a hotel-casino, which obviously benefits from having potential gamblers on its premises.

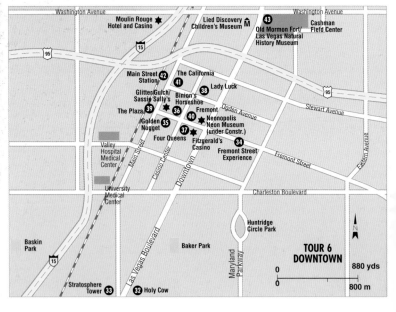

GAMBLING BEGAN HERE

The main Downtown area of Las Vegas is centered around **Fremont Street**, the place where Nevada gambling began. Fremont Street, now nearly 100 years old, was the site of the first Las Vegas traffic signal; the city's first paved street; and its first telephone. Nevada's first gaming license was issued to the long-defunct Northern Club at 13 E Fremont. The James Bond movie *Diamonds Are Forever* is one of the many films shot on the street over the years.

The city has been vexed over Downtown for years; in fact, ever since the Strip began to draw away all its visitors. 'Las Vegas has its casino corridor but that's not for its residents,' says Bernardo Fort-Brescia, whose architectural firm is busily developing a 64-acre (26-hectare) residential and technology park in Hong Kong. 'Las Vegas is now large and sophisticated enough that it demands a focal point, a sense of place for its residents.' Because of a recent sale of 1,900 acres (770 hectares) by the US Bureau of Land Management – which owns almost all the surrounding territory – a further 5,000 homes are set to go up in North Las Vegas, which abuts on the downtown area.

FREMONT STREET EXPERIENCE

The ★★★ **Fremont Street Experience** ㉞ already covers more than five blocks and is constantly being expanded. Every evening hour (between 6 and 11pm) sightseers cluster in the casino-lined mall to enjoy a computer-generated, high-tech light-and-sound show projected onto a 1,400-ft-long (430-meter) frame, nearly 100 ft (30 meters) overhead.

Overwhelming sound pours from speakers on each block, and the experience – there are many different shows – is sometimes enhanced by street performers in furry animal costumes, theatrical smoke and hypnotic, robotic lights. The balcony at Fitzgerald's is a good viewpoint, although it only has 10 seats so you have to get there early.

The casino, which will give you a free O'Lucky Bucks card to improve your gambling chances,

Star Attraction
● **Fremont Street Experience**

Craps
Craps is derived from an old, well-known British game called hazard. It was given its present name by slaves living in New Orleans in the early 1800s.

Craps

Map on page 64

also gives away posters of the light show. Fremont Street's existing neon throws off enough light to read by, but it's switched off just before each performance. If you happen to be playing the same slot machine regularly – anticipating an eventual payoff – keep your eye on it as you walk outside to watch the show, because there are bettors who are awaiting just such a chance to take over your odds-friendly slot.

> **The die is cast**
> All four US companies that make dice can craft them to a tolerance of one ten-thousandth of an inch (two thousandths of a millimeter.) If requested, they can also insert barely visible security symbols.

Roll, baby, roll

DOWNTOWN'S MOVING PICTURES

After an opening fanfare, the latticework ceiling over the five-block pedestrian mall unveils a spectacular moving picture show, in which cartoon characters and amusing animals dance to country and western music, sometimes triggering impromptu dancing by couples in the street. A herd of buffalo stampede overhead, followed by a batch of screaming jet fighters trailing smoke behind them; a tropical jungle with exotic birds and flora segues into a space odyssey, followed by animated instruments, thunder and lightning or twin rows of lovely ladies dancing to a samba beat. There is loud applause and cheers as the show ends.

The annual $6 million cost of operating the Fremont Street mall, which uses 2 million lights and 208 speakers in the experience, is shared by Downtown casinos, which contributed over one-third of the initial $70 million of the project's cost. An equal amount was kicked in by the Downtown Redevelopment Agency. At one time, four out of five visitors to Las Vegas went Downtown, but in recent years this figure had declined to less than one in five.

Free parking is offered to visitors with validation from any of the main Downtown casinos. 'Our intent is to have people realize that if you come Downtown, you're going to see something different,' says Don Snyder, who headed the project.

Work has begun, but temporarily halted in that infuriating Vegas way, on an extension to the Fremont Street spectacle. **Neonopolis** is a shopping and restaurant complex which will eventually include a **Neon Museum** housing colorful signs from a glitzy, earlier era. Some of these are already on display along the street.

For architect Jon Jerde, the Fremont Street Experience is just one example of his quest to bring style to the ongoing malling of America. All his previous endeavors have broken new ground, including the security-conscious Universal City Walk – which has become a major tourist draw in Los Angeles.

When he finished designing another such project, San Diego's spacey Horton Plaza, he explained: 'We have to understand that retail is the last vestige of communal life in America. If we want to save community life in our country, we have to concentrate to a large degree on changing the places where we shop. I don't consider what I design in the strictest sense malls. I'm designing the Main Streets and public squares of the 21st century.'

Below: Downtown attraction
Bottom: Fremont Street Experience

VEGAS VILLAGE

Urban downtown areas are in trouble everywhere, and Las Vegas is no exception, with the proposed Neonopolis being just the latest concept to woo the crowds. 'When I came here in 1964,' says the city's effervescent mayor Oscar Goodman, 'we had a place called Vegas Village, a marketplace

Map
on page
64

Below and bottom: four casinos meet at this intersection

where everyone came and did their shopping. The politicians were there, the gangsters, the actors. That's the kind of feel I want to reinvent for Downtown.'

Unfortunately, there is no general agreement on how to effect this revival. Some think that only the kind of big buildings and glitz that pulls tourists to the Strip will do the trick; others want Downtown to develop in a small-scale fashion from what's already there – evoking 'a neon, desert version of New Orleans, naughty but eminently livable' as *Las Vegas Life* puts it.

GOLDEN NUGGET

There are four casinos at the main intersection, consisting of Fremont Street and Casino Center Boulevard, but the ★★ **Golden Nugget** ❸ stands out against the neon crassness of its neighbors, with its classy white exterior trimmed with soft gold lights. The Golden Nugget has retained the Victorian style that it displayed when it first opened as a saloon 50 years ago, an era when horses could still be seen on the streets. Crystal chandeliers reflect off polished brass and marble in the lobby. Brass and granite squares shine from the surrounding sidewalk. Its buffet always has long lines, especially for Sunday's very popular champagne brunch.

In 1972, Steve Wynn continued his meteoric career in gambling at the Golden Nugget, becoming at 31 the youngest corporate chairman in the history of Las Vegas. He added hotel rooms and suites, of which there are now almost 2,000. An outdoor pool sits in landscaped gardens with tall palm trees; the terrace is lined with white alabaster swans and sculptures of bronze fish. In the Spa Suite Tower, the **Grand Court** is modeled on a room in the Frick Museum of New York, and on display in the casino itself is **the world's largest gold nugget**, weighing a staggering 59.84 lb (27.2 kg). Called the Hand of Faith, the nugget was discovered in Australia. One of the casino shows features country and western lookalikes, which is almost as popular as the visits to view the nugget.

BINION'S HORSESHOE

Big bucks have for a long time been associated with ★ **Binion's Horseshoe** ❸❻, which originally opened as the Eldorado Club in 1937. It gained fame from a display of $1 million in $10,000 bills in a bullet-proof glass display case, beside which 150,000 visitors a year were photographed. (It was free but, of course, it entailed a wait in the casino until the photo was ready.) The display has now been removed and nothing has taken its place, although Binion's has retained its reputation as a gambling favorite.

There's a legendary story about a man who once came into the casino with two suitcases, opened one and converted the $770,000 it contained into chips, which he deposited on the pass line at a nearby craps table. The gambler made his point, doubled his money and cashed in. He used the second suitcase to carry out his winnings.

The annual **World's Poker Series** is hosted by Binion's Horseshoe mid-April to mid-May, offering $10 million in prizes, including $1 million for the world champion – prizes big enough to entice 4,000 gamblers. Started in 1970 by Benny Binion, the tournament outgrew the casino, and so Benny bought another of the four corner casinos, The Mint, which had a small rooftop swimming pool and a huge illuminated clock, the only one that can be seen Downtown. Gradually the

Star Attraction
● Golden Nugget

Multi-dollar bet
According to local reports, only one $1 million bet has ever been placed in a Las Vegas casino. A man bet $1 million on the craps table at Binion's Horseshoe — and lost.

Binion's Horseshoe

Smoking

Sin City casts a benevolent eye on smokers, which cannot be said of anywhere else in America. Several casinos have their own designated cigar lounges, while others sell cigars and leave their customers to find their own comfortable spot. In Downtown's Main Street station, inhalers can partake of their 'hobby' in a beautiful Pullman Railroad car built during the heyday of smoking, in 1927, while an emerging trend is a social event that combines cigar smoking with an evening meal or drinks and hors d'oeuvres. These entertaining evenings are called, of course, 'smokers.'

Everybody wants to be one of these

tournament has been broadened so that now some competitions cost less than a dime to enter. Unfortunately for would-be world champions, the value of money is always minimized by gamblers: 'a dime' means a thousand dollars, 'a nickel' refers to a $5 chip and a quarter represents $25. 'A dollar straight' is a hundred-dollar bill. The lowest entry price in the tournament is $220.

FREE FOOD AND DRINK

The Horseshoe, whose carpets are patterned with the crossed-T brand used on the family's cattle ranch in Montana, offers late-night gamblers a complete New York Steak Dinner for around $5 (10pm–5.45am), which the *Las Vegas Advisor* called 'the greatest LV meal deal of all time.' Downtown's older casinos have always had to battle to woo customers away from the more glamorous Strip, so they give free food to almost three quarters of their visitors. In contrast, the Strip casinos give almost half their customers free drinks, which is a slightly better ratio than you will find Downtown.

The two other corners of the Fremont and Casino Center intersection are occupied by what's still called Sam Boyd's Fremont casino, and the Four Queens casino, which promotes both 'the world's largest blackjack table' (seats 12 gamblers at a time) and the world's largest slot machine (which can be played by six people).

Jimmy 'The Scot' Jordan gives free one-hour lessons on how to win at various games three times a day at the ★ **Four Queens** 37, and the casino claims that some of its slots have a 97.4 percent payback, which is a little better than the Downtown average of 95.6 percent. Downtown slots, according to *Casino Player*'s Jim Hildebrand, pay back almost 2 percent more than the 25¢ machines on the Strip. However, the biggest gambling bargain at such Downtown casinos as Binion's, **El Cortez** or the **Golden Gate** are the 25¢ craps tables, often with drinks thrown in for free. Don't forget to tip the waitress.

Because Las Vegas casinos collectively clear

profits of about $17 million each day, they don't
balk at giving away about $2 million a day in
comps: free rooms, shows, dining or plays. The
easiest route for their munificence is via slot clubs
whose members – and that could include you –
carry cards that rack up points each time they
are used, irrespective of wins or losses.

The points, which can be exchanged for all
kinds of favors, add up remarkably fast, given the
addictive way most people charge around Las
Vegas – and what the casino gets out of it, of
course, is that the cards keep you coming back.

Below: cowgirl with altitude
Bottom: free lessons here

GLITTER GULCH

Other attractions in the Fremont Street mall
include **Sassy Sally's**, which offers free photos
(you wait in the casino until they're ready) and
250 different beers; **Indian Arts & Crafts**, its
entrance flanked by totem poles; the topless girls
of neon-blazing **Glitter Gulch**, the entrance to
which is guarded by intimidating doormen who
demand to see identification no matter what your
age; and **Fitzgerald's Casino**, with a McDonald's
outlet in a quieter corner.

Across the street is a store with every kind of
souvenir, including chopped-up dollars in a bottle, miniature slot machines and T shirts with slo-
gans such as *'If I can't win, I don't want to play.'*

Map
on page
64

LUCK BE A LADY

One block away, on 3rd Street, the Mad Money Slot Players at **Lady Luck** ㊳ can get complimentary rooms, limo transfers and arena seats in the casino's private box for rodeos, concerts and sports events. The casino's free 'funbook' includes not only a one-night stay but also a free long-distance phone call. Another way a casino increases loyalty is to offer free membership to its own personal club. Members get a card which they can then insert into the slot machines.

Below: slots in the dark
Bottom: wheel of fortune

The card allows them to play for credit, but it also tracks them, creating a database of how much and how often they gamble. 'They are not all good players, but at least I've got their names,' says Alain J. Uboldi, President and CEO of the Lady Luck Gaming Corp. Even small-time players at Uboldi's casino get such rewards as $10 a night rooms or 1–2 percent of their gambling money returned in gifts or favors.

Towering ahead at the end of Fremont Street is **The Plaza** ㊴, which on Friday evenings sponsors a promotion called Jive at 5, a street party with music and $1 drinks hosted by the dancers from the hotel's *Naked Angels* show. Behind the Plaza are railroad tracks, currently used only by freight trains, although it is frequently said that the once-popular passenger service to Los Angeles will run on its tracks again.

MAIN STREET CASINOS

Almost opposite on Main Street are two casinos, **The Fremont ⑩** and **The California ⑪**. They are part of the Boyd chain whose founder, Sam Boyd, emigrated from Oklahoma in the Depression years and learned his trade while working on gambling ships off the California coast. He died aged 81 in 1995, and many of the multi-million dollar Boyd Gaming Corporation's employees are stockholders.

Owner of The Stardust hotel on the Strip, Boyd's company bought the Main Street Station casino opposite the California and reopened it. Now adjoining it is the **Triple7 BrewPub**, Downtown's only micro brewery, which produces a range of beers from light German ale to dark malty Porter. In the bar, TV screens show sports and music videos, and the pub serves food from lunch through to late-night suppers.

Main Street Station ⑫ takes pride in recreating 1900-era 'turn-of-the-century opulence.' Some of the stained glass windows (surprisingly underlit) were originally given to Lillian Russell by Diamond Jim Brady, and the beveled glass panels came from the actress's Pittsburgh mansion. There are 1870 street lamps from Belgium, century-old chandeliers from both the Paris and San Francisco opera houses, plus bronze doors from a Kuwait bank.

BUFFALO BILL

Along the sidewalk, passers-by can peer into a beautifully preserved **Pullman railroad car**, in which Buffalo Bill Cody lived as he toured the country a century ago, its antique-filled guest quarters once occupied (separately) by Teddy Roosevelt and Annie Oakley.

A little north of the downtown area, at the corner of Las Vegas Boulevard North and Washington Avenue, lies another bit of the old Wild West: reconstruction work continues on the historic **Old Mormon Fort ⑬**, which was built by Brigham Young's pioneers in 1855 to protect missionaries and settlers en route to California.

> **Gamblers' bookstore**
> The Gamblers' Bookshop has stood for almost 30 years at the corner of Charleston Boulevard and 11th Street. In addition to more than 1,000 titles on gambling (and such related subjects as the Mafia), manager Howard Schwartz keeps adding files on everything from card tricks to slot machine crooks. If a book on a subject doesn't exist, Howard tries to find a suitable writer to produce it. 'I have a lot of respect for people who buy books so they can understand the games,' he says. 'Knowing what you're doing allows you to slow down your losses.' Fledgling gamblers who don't bother to educate themselves 'might as well mail their wallets in.'

The Plaza

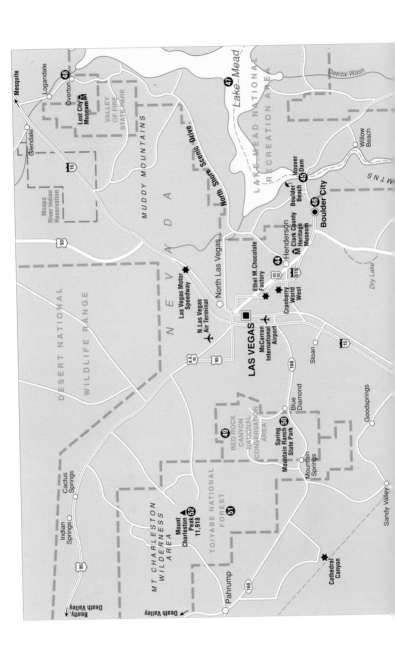

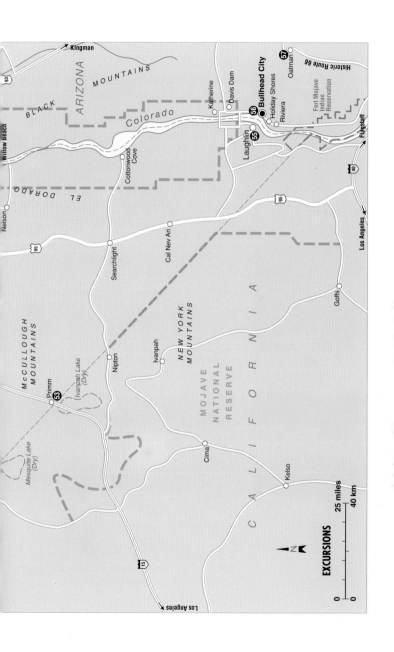

Map
on pages
74–5

Visiting the Dam
Visitors who would like to know more about hydro-electric power generation can join a 35-minute guided tour through the generator halls at the base of Hoover Dam. The dam provides much of the electricity for Nevada, Arizona and Southern California.

Cruising Lake Mead

Excursion 1

Henderson – Hoover Dam – Boulder City – Lake Mead – Overton – Valley of Fire

The most popular day trip from Las Vegas is to Lake Mead and Hoover Dam, 25 miles (40 km) to the southeast of town. En route, a stop can be made at **Henderson 44**, a community in the making that will be the second largest city in Nevada by the year 2010. It was recently listed third out of 187 places by a magazine that rates retirement communities. There are a few free attractions in Henderson that make it worth a stop, but be careful – a great deal of Henderson's sprawl is undeveloped, and it is easy to get lost.

CHOCOLATE AND CLOWNS

A left turn off US 95, onto Russell Road and down Mountain Vista, brings you to the **Ethel M Chocolate Factory** (2 Cactus Garden Drive, tel: 888/627-0990), that offers free tours of the factory where some of the world's most famous candy is made (M & Ms, Snickers, Milky Way and Mars Bars). The factory grounds also have an attractive cactus garden.

Continue down Sunset Road to Marks, and just past where it meets the Warm Springs Road is **Ron Lee's World of Clowns** (330 Carousel Parkway, tel: 888/434-1700, open Mon–Fri 8.30am–4.30pm) where animation figures are made. Inspect the clown museum, ride the carousel and visit the gift shop.

Back to US 95, a turn to the south at Gibson brings you to American Pacific Drive, along which is **Cranberry World West** (702/566-7160, open 9am–5pm, closed Sun), a manufacturing facility with a museum, demonstration kitchen, juice bar, dancing 'Cran Cran Girl' and a gift shop selling cranberry mustard, cranberry wine etc.

The **Clark County Heritage Museum** (1830 S Boulder Highway, tel: 702/455-7955; daily 9am–4.30pm) features a reconstructed ghost town as well as several historic homes, a mining exhibit and Native American artifacts.

Star Attraction
● Hoover Dam

Four miles (6.5 km) before Hoover Dam, the **Gold Strike Inn and Casino**, in sight of the shores of Lake Mead, has a famous all-you-can-eat crab-leg buffet worth skipping breakfast for, and a glass case of old gaming machines and elaborately designed cash registers. The walls are covered with old billboards advertising long-forgotten products.

HOOVER DAM

Straddling the Arizona–Nevada border, the magnificent ★★★ **Hoover Dam** ⑮, anchored to the rugged volcanic walls of **Black Canyon**, towers 726 ft (221 meters) above the Colorado River. For years the dam was – and occasionally still is – known as Boulder Dam, because of the unpopularity of President Herbert Hoover, who had largely been responsible for pushing its approval through Congress. The dam is fed by the Rocky Mountain snow fields running into the 1,400-mile (2,250-km) long Colorado River. Lake Mead stretches back from the dam about 100 miles (160 km) to where the Colorado River exits the Grand Canyon. From the dam the river heads south, acting as the state border with Arizona all the way into Lake Mojave, which is blocked at the southern end by Davis Dam.

Dedicated by President Roosevelt in 1935, the Hoover Dam's 17 generators produce enough electricity to power half a million homes every

Below and bottom: the Hoover Dam straddles the border of two states

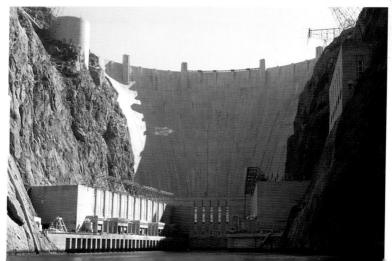

Map on pages 74-5

year. The dam's primary purpose was flood control, but the lake formed by filling a chain of deep canyons now supplies water to nearly 25 million people, including Las Vegans. Even in the 1930s the dam, 45-ft (14-meters) thick at the top, cost $60 million to build (although – to put it into perspective – this is less than 10 percent of the cost of the MGM Grand Hotel).

The dam, 660 ft (200 meters) thick at its base, required 4.4 million cubic yards (3.4 million cubic meters) of concrete. Because of the huge amount of heat generated by concrete as it settles, it was necessary to first pour the concrete into a series of interlocked columns, all inset with miles and miles of tubes through which cooling water flowed. Explanatory films are shown in a theater at the state-of-the-art **Visitor Center** (tel: 702/293-8637).

BOULDER CITY

In **Boulder City** ㊻, the purpose-built community to house the 4,000 workers building the dam, the 12-year construction story is recalled in the **Hoover Dam Museum** (444 Hotel Plaza, tel: 702/294-1988, daily 10am–5pm, Sun noon–5pm). Free walking maps of the historic district (the oldest building is Ira Browder's Cafe, built in 1931) are available at the **Chamber of Commerce** (tel: 702/293-2034) at 1305 Arizona Street.

Boulder Dam Hotel
The Boulder Dam Hotel in Boulder City, the first destination resort in Southern Nevada, has reopened after years of neglect and near-ruin. Built in 1933, when Las Vegas was little more than an arid community, the 22-room hotel flourished at a time when the rich and the famous wanted to see the 'taming of the Colorado River' via the construction of the great dam. Guests included John Wayne, Bette Davis, Shirley Temple and various members of royalty. For information and reservations, tel: 702/293-3510.

Boulder City

LAKE MEAD

★★ **Lake Mead** ❹, with a jagged shoreline of 550 miles (885 km), contains enough water to cover the entire state of New York to a depth of about one foot. Angling goes on year-round but a license is required. The lake has many camping areas, and its recreational area is visited by nine million visitors a year. At the **Lake Mead Marina** (tel: 702/293-6180) or at the dam itself you can take a 90-minute cruise on the *Desert Princess*, a triple-deck paddle wheeler. Visitors to the lake who hang their beer and soda over the side of a boat to cool find the drinks come up warmer – the average daytime temperature of the water is 86°F (30°C) in summer. Nevada Highway 167, which is also called the **North Shore Scenic Drive**, runs for 20 miles (30 km) along the shore, but there are no roads on the south side.

At the northern end of Lake Mead, at the top of what's known as the Overton Arm, is the little town of ★ **Overton** ❹. The **Lost City Museum** is devoted to the history of the Anasazi Indians who lived in the area for centuries, but deserted it as long as 800 years ago, probably due to drought. Ironically, the area the Anasazi once considered home is now covered by the waters of Lake Mead, and the museum contains some of the artifacts (beads, polished shells and bone gambling counters) that were salvaged by archaeologists before the lake and the dam were built.

Overton is about one hour's drive north of Las Vegas, and the fastest route is via Interstate 145 and then southeast on SR 169. But a more rewarding journey is to take the southern access to SR 169, driving the circuitous route through the spectacular **Valley of Fire**, with its intriguing red rock formations, petroglyphs and camping grounds. A useful leaflet is available from the Ranger toll booth at the entrance, and also from the attractive **Visitor Center** about midway through the route.

Take something to drink, as even the center is sometimes without water and contains no soft-drink machines. Spring and fall are the best times to visit: temperatures soar well over 100°F (38°C) in the summer months.

Star Attraction
● Lake Mead

Below and bottom: the liquid attractions of Lake Mead

Map on pages 74–5

Excursion 2

Red Rock Canyon – Mount Charleston

State Highway 159 leads 15 miles west to ★★ **Red Rock Canyon** ㊾, once home to the Paiute Indian tribe where more than 1 million visitors a year pay a small admission fee to admire the wild horses and burros, the desert bighorn sheep, the coyotes and antelope – but most of all the magnificent landscape. A loop trip from Las Vegas covers 39 miles (63 km) and can be made in an afternoon.

Below: Red Rock Canyon
Bottom: bighorn sheep

Terra-Cotta Red

The rocks of the canyon change color as the day progresses, and when the shadows grow long in the evening the canyon turns a deep terra-cotta red. There are plans to double the size of this National Conservation Area to 195,000 acres (79,000 hectares). Red Rock Canyon has sculpted vistas, hidden waterfalls, wandering burros and desert vegetation. There are trails for hikers and cyclists, routes for rock climbers and a scenic drive. The **Visitor Center** (tel: 702/363-1921), which closes at 4:30pm, displays examples of Mojave Desert flora and fauna.

The canyon also has **Bonnie Springs Old Nevada** (tel: 702/875-4191), an old western town with motels, shops and Wild West shoot-outs. It is open until 5pm in winter, till 6pm in summer and there is an admission fee.

Within the Red Rock Canyon Conservation Area is **Spring Mountain Ranch State Park** ㊿, a ranch once owned by Howard Hughes. The millionaire is gone now, but the consequences of his time here carry on. The Howard Hughes Corporation is planning a huge development running at the edge of the area. It will include 18,000 residential units, golf courses, restaurants and possibly a hotel-casino.

Between the canyon and Mount Charleston is 35 miles (56 km) of sagebrush, crimson blooming cactus, yellow wildflowers, glowing sands and the ancient bristle cone pines of the **Toiyabe National Forest** (51) (parking fee) where elk and other wildlife roam. **Mount Charleston** 🐂, which peaks at 11,918 feet (3,633 meters) captures enough westerly precipitation to support a varied vegetation, with 30 species of plants endemic to the region.

The mountain is high enough to support both summer and winter activities. The area is popular for skiing and sleigh rides in winter, and horse rides, wagon rides and hiking in the summer. There are plans to build a golf resort costing around $35 million near the pleasantly rural **Mount Charleston Hotel** (tel: 702/872-5500) where a roaring fireplace dominates the huge lobby. There is an adjoining nine-hole golf course.

ON TO DEATH VALLEY

Continuing north on US 95, after 100 miles (160 km) of unpopulated, mostly barren terrain, you come to the small town of **Beatty**. Here, State 190 leads past the ruins of **Rhyolite**, which was a prosperous mining community at the turn of the 19th century but is now a ghost town. Every spring there's a Resurrection festival at which participants dress in period costumes. The highway continues west for many desolate miles right through the heart of **Death Valley**, from which it emerges to join US 395 at Olancha. (For more on Death Valley, *see Insight Compact Guide: California*.)

Star Attraction
● **Red Rock Canyon**

👁 **Desert Travel**
Driving in the desert can be a hazardous experience, and should not be undertaken lightly. But most motorists will be fine if they remember these rules:
● fill up your gas tank
● carry a spare can of gas in the trunk
● check the tires of your car
● carry lots of water, and drink often
● wear a sunhat, glasses and screen
● tell someone your destination
● travel with a good map.

Mount Charleston biking

Map on pages 74–5

Excursion 3

Primm (Stateline) – Jean

The most dramatic sight on the desert route to or from Las Vegas are the lights of ★ **Primm ㊾**, the three-hotel community that sits just across the Nevada border into California. The 'town', formerly called Stateline, can be seen so far ahead (at the bottom of a long steep hill) that most drivers stop if only out of curiosity and for many it's an irresistible stopover, leaving the last 43 miles (70 km) to Las Vegas for the next morning.

Primm's trio of casinos are linked by monorail; the resorts on the east side of Interstate 15 and Whiskey Pete's on the west side are known as the **Primadonna Casino Resorts**, now owned by the MGM-Mirage company.

OLD WESTERN STYLE

Buffalo Bill's is a maze of corridors connecting 614 rooms, and it is very popular. There is a busy check-in line even at midnight. The interior is heavy on Old Western style, with a Hangman's Bar and the start of a themed log-flume ride. The logs float past stuffed animals – a vulture perches overhead – and animatronic old prospectors. There is an eye-popping buggy ride in a motion simulator across bumpy desert trails, which is terrific.

Gas up first
The gas stations in the town of Primm do not display their prices out front, which means they can charge pretty much what they like. So be sure to gas up before you set out.

Primm Valley Golf Club

There's also an arena for concerts, a bowling alley, a movie theater, a golf course and a couple of restaurants. It's a short walk or ride between Buffalo Bill's and **Whisky Pete's**, allegedly named after an old character who ran a gas station here long ago. The RV park has 200 hook-ups, and is very popular.

BONNIE AND CLYDE

Inside the **Primm Valley Resort and Casino** (which has a famous golf course) is an exhibit which includes the bullet-scarred Ford V8 in which runaway gangsters Bonnie and Clyde met their death, as well as Clyde's blood-stained shirt inside a glass case. A letter now adorns the dark-gray Ford that Clyde Barrow had stolen in Topeka, Kansas, a few weeks earlier.

Below: roller coaster in Primm
Bottom: fashion outlet

'While I still have breath in my lungs,' Clyde scrawled in a letter to Henry Ford, 'I will tell you what a dandy car you make. I have driven Fords exclusively when I could get away with one. For sustained speed and freedom from trouble, the Ford has got every other car skinned.' One month after mailing this note, on May 23, 1934, Bonnie and Clyde were at last ambushed by the police – who had been pursuing them through most of the states west of the Mississippi River after a series of bank raids – and killed by one or more of the many bullets that riddled the vehicle. Two bodies, 15 guns and 168 rounds of ammunition were recovered from the Ford when the shooting finally stopped.

Primm's ★ **Fashion Outlet Las Vegas** has discount shops selling fashions by upscale designers like Calvin Klein, Versace, Ralph Lauren and others. A bus runs from the New York, New York casino on Las Vegas's Strip. Call 702/874-1400 for a schedule of times.

Back on Interstate 15 heading east, you can stop at the town of **Jean** ㊴, 34 miles (55 km) short of Las Vegas, which has two major casinos – the **Nevada Landing** (tel: 800/628-6682) and the **Gold Strike** (tel: 800/634-1359) – in the form of turn-of-the-19th-century theme hotels.

Excursion 4

Laughlin – Katherine – Oatman

Map
on pages
74–5

Don Laughlin began buying slot machines to install in local bars while he was still at school in Minnesota, so his eventual move to Nevada seems almost predictable. In 1966 he paid $235,000 for 6 acres (2.4 hectares) located on the **Colorado River** where it separates the states of Nevada and Arizona. He built an 8-room motel and began by offering all-you-can-eat chicken dinners for 98¢. Today, the tiny motel – which had originally become popular during the construction of the Boulder (Hoover) Dam – has now grown into the 1,405-room, 93-suite Riverside Resort.

Fishing

Fishing in the Colorado River is a popular sport. Local fish include Largemouth Bass; Channel Catfish; Crappie, Rainbow Trout; Blue Gill, and two endnagered species, the Razorback Sucker and the Bonytail Chub. A license is required for anyone over 14 years of age, but a 3-day permit can be bought at any one of a number of places in Laughlin or Bullhead City. For more information tel: 800/275-3474 or 800/ASK-FISH.

A TOWN OF ONE'S OWN

When a US Postal Service inspector insisted the fledgling town be given a name, the entrepreneur followed the official's advice and gave it his own family name, ★ **Laughlin** ⑤⑤. This decision is indicative of his business philosophy. 'The Riverside is a friendly, family operation,' he says. 'We are the natural heir to a market that corporations alienate.'

Catch of the day

Nevertheless, the corporations against which he contrasts Riverside soon became aware of the six-million annual visitors to the town, and staked out their own claims along a river bank where land has cost as much as $1.5 million an acre ($3.7 million a hectare). The **Golden Nugget** (2300 Casino Drive, tel: 702/298-7222 or 800/950-7700 with its lush tropical garden, is sister to its namesake in Las Vegas. **The Edgewater** (tel: 702/298-2453 or 800/252-8445), where some jackpots pay off in silver coins, and the *Colorado Belle* (2100 S. Casino Drive, tel: 702/298-4000 or 800/47-RIVER), with its paddle-steamer design, are owned by Mandalay Resorts Group.

Harrah's (2900 S. Casino Drive, tel: 702/298-4600 or 800/447-8700), with a private beach, and the **Flamingo Hilton** (1900 Casino Drive, tel: 702/298-5111 or 800/352-6464) are both related to their Las Vegas namesakes. And the **Ramada**

Express casino (tel: 702/298-4200 or 888/872-4605) operates a steam locomotive on a mile-long track to shuttle customers to and from the busy parking lot.

DOWN BY THE RIVERSIDE

There are now almost a dozen hotel-casinos beside the Colorado River, all connected by a **River Walk** and a riverboat service operating as a water taxi. **The River Palms** , formerly the Gold River, (2700 Casino Drive, tel: 702/298-2242 or 800/835-7903) has the only 24-hour buffet, in addition to a gourmet restaurant set around pine trees and a stream. All the establishments have nightly entertainment and plenty of good eating places: window-side diners at the Riverside and the Flamingo can watch the ferries on the river, and the Ramada has a steak house located in a Victorian-era parlor car

Below: Laughlin river flight
Bottom: alternative transportation

When it came to shooting the movie *Leaving Las Vegas*, the producers chose Laughlin as a set because they thought it more relaxed than Vegas itself. Much of the film was shot in the River Palms, which has just imported enough sand to create a 300-ft (90-meter) beach.

Special events in Laughlin tend to be fairly *macho*, shows like 600 cowboys competing in five days of rodeo events such as riding, roping

Map
on pages
74–5

and bull wrestling with 'western entertainment' thrown in, are on offer in late March, while top bull riders compete for a $100,000 purse at the Laughlin Shoot-Out in September. There is speed-boat racing on the Colorado River in early June, and thousands of leather-jacketed motor-cycle enthusiasts turn up for a 'rumble in the desert' every year in late April.

Back in the founding **Riverside Resort** (1650 Casino Drive, tel: 702/298-2535 or 800/227-3849) are half a dozen movie theaters and a classic car collection. Restaurants are supplied with steaks from the Laughlin family's ranch in the Hualapai Mountains The family company also owns the River Queen Motel (located across the river in Bullhead, Arizona, tel: 800/227-3849), which is connected to the Riverside by a free shuttle boat. Rooms are considerably cheaper in Laughlin than in Las Vegas, dropping to a low of about $15 per person in the blisteringly hot summer months and invariably staying below $25 per person except for holiday weekends and whenever there is a convention in town.

Below: Laughlin Shoot-Out
Bottom: beauties and the Belle

NATIVE AMERICAN CASINO

Until the casino era, the debilitating heat kept down the region's population which from the earliest days had consisted mostly of Mojave Indians, the

only people who learned to adjust to the unpredictable river's flow – sometimes shriveling to a trickle in summer, sometime swelling to a raging torrent that ravaged their crops. At a settlement called Katherine, just north of Laughlin, a gold mine operated from about 1900 and produced $12 million of ore until it closed in 1942. Steamboats operated on the river, delivering supplies to the miners and returning filled with the precious metal. In the previous century, sternwheelers operated from what is now the town of **Bullhead City** 56, charging travelers $44 for a trip that first headed south, then transfered to a coach bound for San Francisco.

As in other parts of the US, Native Americans are looking to gather some of the astonishing profits to be made from gambling. **The Avi** (1000 Aha Macay Parkway, tel: 702/535-5555 or 800-284-2946), 9 miles (15 km) southwest of Laughlin, is run by the Fort Mojave tribe. The hotel was the first Indian-owned casino in Nevada, and it has a Southwestern and Indian theme. In the tribal language of the Fort Mojave Indian, the name of the casino, Avi, means 'something of value'.

Star Attraction
● Route 66

Route 66
Route 66, also known as the 'Mother Road' is the US's most famous highway. The 2,448-mile (3,940 km) road begins in Chicago, and ends near Los Angeles, passing through eight states, three time zones, and some of the best small towns in America. In fact, another of its nicknames is 'America's Main Street'. Its heyday was the 1940s and '50s, a time which old-timers and nostalgia buffs recall with fondness, remembering the quirky motels, drive-in movie theaters and mom 'n' pop diners, a few of which still remain along the route.

ROUTE 66

A popular excursion from Laughlin is to the town of ★ **Oatman** 57, Arizona, about 25 miles (40 km) southeast, traveling on America's much-feted highway, ★★★ **Route 66**. Oatman looks exactly the way you'd imagine an old western town to look, with sagging wooden shacks lining the lone, unpaved road on which rowdy mock-gunfights are staged most days.

Movie stars Clark Gable and Carole Lombard spent their honeymoon at the worn and characterful (1902) **Oatman Hotel** (tel: 520/768-4408), after having married in nearby **Kingman**. Room 15 is preserved as a sort of shrine to the couple. The 'honeymoon suite' and the 'ghost's room' cost a little extra to stay in, but there is a cozy, local atmosphere in the bar downstairs. Be aware that it can be difficult to get food in Oatman after 5pm, once most tourists have left town.

Kingman and Mother Road

Architecture and Ambiance

It's easy to knock the culture in Las Vegas, but it's impossible to deny its attraction. People flock to Las Vegas in droves. It is a global synonym for glitzy highlife. As one noted observer put it: 'We are all members of the lost tribe of Elvis, wandering here to his neon desert in record droves.' Las Vegas has learned how to package fantasy like no other place on earth, and it does it with architecture and design.

PACKAGING FANTASY

The core product of Las Vegas is still gambling, but the packaging is threatening to take over. Many people would argue that the architecture of the town plays an increasingly significant role in its success, although, as one magazine writer recently observed, it's 'performance architecture' that we enjoy less for its realism than its ingenuity. Ironically, with every eye-popping new structure and revamp that brings in fresh crowds, there are others who abhor the changes.

Joyce Orias, who works for the interior design firm that remodeled Caesars Palace, says it has been controversial because there were some old venues that people went to on their honeymoon and their annual vacation for years after. 'And they're complaining that they're not there any-more – 'what's happened to this place?' they cry.'

Nevertheless, Dave Hickey, professor of art criticism and theory at the University of Nevada Las Vegas, says: 'All the problems that architects had to face with building on the Strip were problems of scale. It's the only place in the world where they try to make buildings look smaller.'

Las Vegas has done a lot to change people's perceptions about what is acceptable in architecture. Even in its early days as a gambling resort in the 1940s and '50s, the casino builders were willing to take chances with the outré, hiring the same architects responsible for the unconventional drive-in coffee shops that were defining the ambiance of Los Angeles.

> **Neon history**
> British dentist Sir William Ramsey is credited with discovering the inert gas known as neon in 1898. A decade later a Frenchman, Georges Claude, created the familiar glow by inserting an electrode into a tube of the gas. In 1923, a Packard car dealer lit up his Wilshire Boulevard showroom in Los Angeles, while six years later Thomas Young brought neon to Vegas with a sign in his Fremont Street casino, the Oasis Club. Downtown has long been associated with blazing light: the 'Vegas Vic' sign and the neon cowgirl above Glitter Gulch are icons around the world.

Opposite: Paris in the sand
Below: Neon Museum exhibit

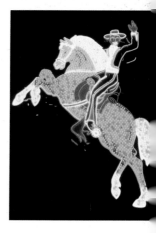

Ultimate Buildings

Architects often either desire to build in a new way or strive to replicate classic styles. But in Las Vegas more than anywhere else, architects aim to do both at the same time in their own inimitable way. 'We have an obligation to stretch our imagination, to build the ultimate buildings,' says Weldon Simpson, the Luxor's architect. 'Civilizations are noted for their architecture, and when future archaeologists dig up Las Vegas they will see a civilization that had the imagination and energy to go beyond what had ever been done before.'

Viva Las Venice

It would be rash to predict that Sin City architects had anywhere near exhausted their visions for spectacular new casinos: San Francisco, London and the Orient are ideas still floating around for future projects, for example. But one of the newer trends, it seems, is the race to build ever-more imaginative shopping areas of the type for which the simple word 'mall' is totally inadequate. Top of the current list (though, alas, not in sales) is the sensational Desert Passage, adjoining the Aladdin Hotel.

Here, shops are tucked into a towering eight-story mountainside, and lining a North African harbor front, complete with full-size freighter, where a mock storm with thunder, lightning and rain erupts every hour. A so-called Lost City is modeled after the legendary Petra. And at the Grand Canal Shoppes in the nearby Venetian, many months went into creating the frescoed ceiling – an exact copy of a 16th-century work by Paolo Veronese.

The interior of casinos gets as much attention as the outside. Here, as everywhere, color plays a big part. The Stardust, for example, is identified with persistent purple – a sort of imperial trademark. Most casinos use colors to mark them out in this garish crowd. Raul R. Rodriguez has designed hundreds of floats for Pasadena's Rose Parade. When he was called in to renovate the Flamingo Hilton, he gave it off-white walls with splashes of high-energy orange, red, fuschia and yellow. And one cynic wrote that the MGM Grand is green – not just because it's the color of the

Wizard of Oz's Emerald City – but also because it's the color of money. Once you choose your color, you have to find enough space to display it. Designer Charles Silverman of Yates-Silverman Inc. points out that the main things you see in the casino are the floor and the ceiling. 'You have to get the main design impact from the carpet,' says Silverman, who has been designing casino interiors for 35 years, and has the Luxor and the Excalibur to his credit.

THEATRICAL COSTUMES

Another free space on which to brand a casino with innovative design is the employees' uniforms. As you might expect in Las Vegas, these owe more to theatrical costumes than the hotel industry. Joan Poggioli of the New York design company that bears her name explains: 'We have to cater to a broad range of figures. Real people, not models, wear these clothes. We build in adjustable features like Velcro waistbands.'

For similar reasons, the gold shoe-buckles at Treasure Island come with adjustable elastic bands. Costumes are made from lightweight brocades and polyester-cotton blends. 'People have to work in these costumes, they perspire,' Poggioli says. His company created the costumes for the 7,000 employees of the Luxor and Excalibur hotels.

Venice dreams
The Venetian casino was conceived by Sheldon Adelson, the son of a Boston cabbie, and partly financed with the proceeds from the sale of his computer enterprise, COMDEX. After their marriage in 1991, Adelson and his wife Miriam, an Israeli doctor, spent their honeymoon in Venice, then commissioned historians to compile a photo catalogue of artwork and architectural details. 'We think New York-New York [casino] did a fabulous job,' says Adelson, 'but we believe it is a *faux* New York City. We're building what is essentially the *real* Venice.'

Moroccan fantasy

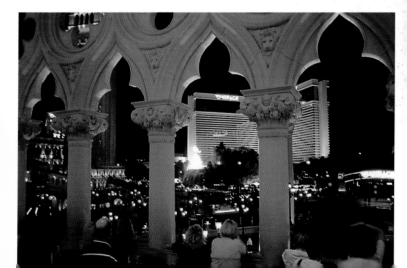

The Treasure Island doorman wears a Captain Hook costume that originally cost $2,000, and is dry-cleaned daily. The cleaning regime is essential. Alan Lurie works for a Chicago design company that creates uniforms for several of the Las Vegas hotels. He says that, with luck and daily cleaning, each uniform should last about a year. Employees typically have three changes of work clothes – 'one on the back, one on the rack and one at the cleaner's.

Is it architecture?
'It's almost silly to walk around a casino and say "is this accurate?", says Richard A. Fazzini, head of Brooklyn Museum's Egyptian and Classical Department.

Fazzini was talking about the Luxor hotel, which he says is the heir to a long line of Egyptian-influenced buildings, both in the US and in other countries. These buildings include museums, libraries, insurance offices, Masonic halls, and even prisons.

In Vegas, reality and fantasy are usually blurred

THE TOTAL EXPERIENCE

When all this effort comes together, you have the total Las Vegas experience – a fantasy world where the boundaries with reality are totally and completely blurred. Aaron Betsky argues that in other places, the shopping malls and theaters where you fantasize are carefully isolated from the rest of the world.

But Las Vegas condenses and transforms these experiences into a cacophony of sights and sounds. Your dreams are constantly interrupted by the honking of horns, the jostling of other theatergoers and the sight of left-over souvenir shops, motels and liquor stores swamped by newer, larger spectacles. 'This uncontrolled rag-tag scenery is what keeps the Strip from becoming another Disneyland with dice.'

Museums

Despite Las Vegas's reputation, there are a few places that stimulate the intellect and not just the bank balance. Visitors who feel their brains might need exercising should check out the following:

Below: Natural History Museum exhibit
Bottom: beating the drum for the African-American Museum

Howard W. Cannon Aviation Museum, McCarran Airport, tel: 261-5211. Named after the band leader turned senator who helped establish Nellis Air Force Base, this tells the story of aviation in southern Nevada. Open 24 hours a day.

Las Vegas Art Museum, 9600 W. Sahara Ave, tel: 360-8000. Housed in the Sahara West Fine Arts Building, this is the largest art museum in Nevada, and focuses on contemporary art. There's also a desert sculpture garden and a good collection of African art. Open daily 10am–5pm, Sun 1–5pm, closed Mon.

Las Vegas Natural History Museum, 900 Las Vegas Blvd N, tel: 384-3466. Stuffed birds and dinosaur exhibits centered around a huge shark tank. Open daily 9am–4pm.

Marjorie Barrick Museum of Natural History, University of Nevada at Las Vegas campus, tel: 895-3381. Comprehensive bird collection as well as Nevada's state fossil, the *ichthyosaur*. Open weekdays 9am–4.45pm, Sat 10am–2pm.

Nevada State Museum and Historical Society, 700 Twin Lakes Dr, tel: 486-5205. Mammoths and other ancient beasts, plus how they survived in the desert. Open daily 9am–5pm

Nevada Test Site, Frenchman Flat, tel: 295-1000. Group tours of the Department of Energy's site of the first nuclear test (1951), west of town.

Walker African-American Museum, 705 W. Van Buren Ave, tel: 647-2242. Thousands of dolls, books, figurines, autographs and records. Call for an appointment.

FOOD AND DRINK

The tradition of the Las Vegas buffet began in the 1940s at the original El Rancho Vegas Hotel on the Strip, when the new owner, Beldon Katleman, introduced an "all you can eat for a dollar" Midnight Chuck Wagon Buffet, in an attempt to keep customers in the casino after the second show ended. The idea was copied by other casinos, who gradually extended it to breakfast, lunch and dinner.

Buffets are now standard in virtually all casinos, and studies show that 80 per cent of visitors indulge in buffet food. Typically, selections run to at least 40 or 50 items – salads, fruits, roast beef, baked ham, roast turkey, fried chicken, vegetables, coffee and an exciting array of desserts. Although subject to change, the average prices today are $7 for breakfast, $9 for lunch and $13 for dinner, although during the night many hotels offer bacon-and-egg breakfasts for just a dollar or two.

BUFFETS IN CASINOS

Circus Circus serves more than 10,000 people a day via three serving lines. (Its record is 17,600 diners on one busy day.) **The Excalibur's** buffet dining room, which is full much of the time, seats 1,400 people, and, when combined with its other eating places, serves well over 10 million meals a year. The 200 items in the buffet at the Stardust's **Coco Palms** are derived from almost a dozen ethnic cuisines. **Le Village Buffet** at Paris Las Vegas offers dishes from each of the five French provinces.

The **Carnival World Buffet**, located in the Rio casino, has for years been known for its great-value-for-money meals, with 11 different buffets for one price, including a choice between Mexican, Mongolian grill, Chinese, American and Italian food.

The Riviera's **World's Fare Buffet** serves a champagne brunch on the weekends. **The Tropicana** has a 'Play and Eat Casino' off the main gaming area, where gamblers can nibble on deli fare or sip cappuccino while sitting at the slots. **Slots-A-Fun**, adjoining Circus Circus, has a food bar just inside the door offering a choice of grilled chicken items, burgers, fish and fries – all for around $5.

UPSCALE DINING IN CASINOS

'This is a boomtown and the opportunities are endless,' remarked Tom Kaplan, the partner of Wolfgang Puck in **Spago**, tel: 369-6300, in the Forum at Caesars Palace. Puck was one of the first of the celebrity chefs to reconize the potential of Las Vegas. He has recently opened **Trattoria del Lupo** (tel: 740-5522) in the Mandalay Bay; is involved at **Cili Season** (tel: 856-1000), at the posh Bali Hai Golf Club, and is scheduled to open another restaurant, Postrio, soon.

> **Dining with the stars**
> The restaurant with the best view is the Top of the World, tel: 383-5326, which revolves 360° each hour at the top of the Stratosphere Tower. For diners more interested in good food than good views, two restaurants named after legendary French artists – Picasso at The Bellagio, tel: 693-7223, and Renoir at The Mirage, tel: 791-7223 – are among only 18 restaurants in North America to achieve Mobil five-star award ratings. New York is the only city with more than two highly rated Mobil-starred restaurants. Booking is essential.

Opposite: Bellagio's Circo restaurant

Big night out
All the big casinos have a range of half a dozen restaurants, invariably promoted with the names of their famous chefs (who aren't necessarily in town). The food and the ambiance are usually first-rate – as is the price– but for space reasons we've picked just one restaurant in a casino. Booking is strongly advised, and patrons tend to dress up.

Here is a list of just a few of the scores of restaurants in Las Vegas. Prices are based on this guide:

$$$	=	expensive
$$	=	moderate
$	=	inexpensive

Andre's French Restaurant
The Monte Carlo
3770 Las Vegas Blvd
Tel: 730-7955
A favorite among discerning diners, with a lounge where cigar smokers are welcome. $$$

Buccaneer Bay Club
Treasure Island
3300 Las Vegas Blvd S
Tel: 894-7111
American-Continental dining as patrons watch pirates sink those darn Brits yet again. $$

Commander's Palace
The Aladdin/Desert Passage
3663 Las Vegas Blvd S
Tel: 892-8272
The original New Orleans restaurant, established in 1880, is a place known far and wide, and locals are proud to have this modern version in their city. Be sure to order bananas Foster. $$$

Emer
MGM Grand
9 Las Vegas Blvd S
Tel: 891-7374

Emeril Lagasse also operates the Venetian's **Delmonico Steakhouse**, but here the accent is on fish and the style very French Quarter. $$$

Le Cirque
The Bellagio
3600 Las Vegas Blvd S
Tel: 693-7223
Sister to the legendary New York restaurant, the cuisine is French and equally famous. $$$

Lutece
The Venetian
3355 Las Vegas Blvd S
Tel: 414-4840
One of the city's best – and priciest – restaurants, with modern decor and to-die-for French menu. $$$

Napa
The Rio
3700 W Flamingo Rd
Tel: 247-7961
French chef Jean-Louis Palladin features rabbit, squab and duck in his California wine country cuisine, and the 40,000-bottle wine cellar entailed a $6 million investment. $$$

Nobu
The Hard Rock Hotel
Tel: 693-5090
One of five of these upmarket Japanese restaurants worldwide; the Kobe beef carpaccio is an irresistible specialty. $$$

Onda
The Mirage
3400 Las Vegas Blvd S
Tel: 791-7223
Todd English (who also brought his hugely popular Boston-based restaurant, **Olives**, to the Bellagio) serves delicious and filling Italian-American cuisine in this Tuscan-style dining room. $$$

Palace Court
Caesars Palace's
3570 Las Vegas Blvd S
Tel: 731-7731
'Decor with character,' says *The Wine Spectator*. The Palace *is* a good place for privacy and nostalgia. $$$

Pietro's
The Tropicana
3801 Las Vegas Blvd S
Tel: 739-2341
Fine gourmet dining in an intimate surrounding. $$

Rotisserie des Artistes
Paris Las Vegas
3655 Las Vegas Blvd S
Tel: 967-7999
This attractive, two-story Art Deco-style dining room specializes in game, seafood and steak roasted in rotisserie ovens. $$$

Rumjungle
Mandalay Bay
3950 Las Vegas Blvd
Tel: 632-7408
Rumjungle's exotic dining choices include fish, fowl and grilled meats that are marinated in fruits, tropical spices and rum. Check out the Martiniquan lamb skewer with green curry coconut glaze. $$$

Sacred Sea
The Luxor
3900 Las Vegas Blvd S
Tel: 262-4000
Tile mosaics, a ship's mast and a crow's nest view of the casino action downstairs, while diners devour prize-winning seafood. $$

NON-CASINO DINING

Cafe Nicole
4760 W Sahara Ave
Tel: 870-7675
Charming courtyard for patio dining, day or night. $$

Chunking
3400 S Jones Blvd
Tel: 871-5551
Hugely popular *dim sum* buffet with a score of tasty choices. $$

Crown and Anchor Pub
1350 E Tropicana Ave
Tel: 739-8676
More than 70 beers, and the best fish and chips in town. $

Golden Steer
308 W Sahara Ave
Tel: 384-4470

A gospel brunch at the House of Blues is not to be missed

Alcohol

Drink is tolerated more readily in Vegas than in most American cities. In many casinos, drinks are free to gamblers, served with panache by good-looking waiters and waitresses who make their living from tips. There's an old legend about the skill with which these canny workers could surreptitiously pick up random $10 bills with the wet underside of their trays, but this seems to be yet another Vegas tall tale, and most are scrupulously honest.

Microbrew fans can sample newly minted beers in the Pub & Brewers at the Monte Carlo, and also at the Triple & Brew Pub in Downtown's Main Street Station. Caesars Palace features the Terraza martini bar where a favorite is the vodka-based drink *Et Tu Brute*. For a taste of vintage Vegas, check out the Laughing Jack, whose neon sign opposite the Mandalay Bay has been attracting passers-by into a friendly bar that dates back to the 1950s. Free snacks most nights, and reduced-price drinks on certain evenings.

Thirty years of serving seafood and tasty steaks. $$

Horn of Africa
1510 Las Vegas Blvd S
Tel: 383-6741
A dozen spicy Ethiopian dishes as well as dancing to East African music. $$

JC Wooloughan
The Regent, 221 N Rampart Blvd
Tel: 869-777
A fun Irish pub with dancing and music. $

Kiefer's Atop the Carriage House
105 E Harmon Ave
Tel: 739-8000
Top-notch food, with impeccable service and a wonderful view of the Strip as well. $$

Lotus of Siam
953 E Sahara Ave
Tel: 753-3033
Gourmet magazine recently called the Siam 'simply the best Thai restaurant in the country.' $$

Marrakech
3900 Paradise Road
Tel: 737-5611
Moroccan food and belly dancing. $$

Mayflower Cuisinier
4750 W Sahara
Tel: 870-8432
Contemporary California-style Chinese cuisine with patio dining. $$

Mediterranean Cafe and Market
4147 S Maryland Parkway
Greek favorites include flaming *saganaki* (fried cheese squares) and *spanakopita* (cheese and spinach pie). Dancing optional. $$

Morton's of Chicago
400 E Flamingo Rd
Tel: 893-0703
Waiters present enormous uncooked steaks for inspection; the Cajun-style sirloin is moderately fiery. $$$

Peppermill Lounge
2985 Las Vegas Blvd S
Tel: 735-4177
The relaxing Fireside Lounge has soft seats by a flaming pool. Open 24 hours. Classy coffee-shop menu. $

Rincon de Buenos Aires
5300 W Spring Mountain Rd
Tel: 257-3331
Try the *parillada,* an enormous sizzling platter of mixed meats, and leave room for the sexy desserts. $$

Rosemary's
8125 W Sahara
Tel: 869-2251

Appealing atmosphere, flawless service and roasted lamb with black olive mashed potatoes. **$$**

Stage Deli of Las Vegas
3500 Las Vegas Blvd S
Tel: 893-4045
For New Yorkers, it's like back home, with its matzo ball soup, cheesecake and half-sour pickles. **$**

Shalimar Fine Indian Cuisine
3900 S Paradise Road
Tel: 796-0302
Tasty chicken and lamb dishes from the tandoori oven. **$$**

The Tillerman
2245 E Flamingo Rd
Tel: 731-4036
Seafood is the main attraction at this family-owned spot that's been round for 20 years. **$$**

DINING DOWNTOWN

Burgundy Room
Lady Luck
206 N 3rd St
Tel: 477-3000
A surprising choice for Downtown; diners are surrounded by an elegant 1930s Parisian atmosphere, influenced by Salvador Dalí. **$$**

Gee Joon
Binion's Horseshoe
128 Fremont St
Tel: 382-1600
A moderately-priced Chinese restaurant open only in the evenings. **$**

Hugo's Cellar
Four Queens
202 Fremont St
Tel: 385-4011
Tucked away Downtown, the restaurant has a romantic, New Orleansy atmosphere. The culinary accent strongly favors seafood. **$$**

Liberty Cafe
White Cross Drugstore
1700 Las Vegas Blvd
Tel: 382-1733
Open 24 hours, the Liberty has been operating for 35 years and has a typical lunch-counter atmosphere. **$**

Overland Stage Cafe
The Fremont Hotel
200 E Fremont St
Tel: 385-3232
Features an inexpensive dinner of two lobster tails and a steak. **$$**

The best Downtown buffets can be found at the **Golden Nugget** (tel: 385-7111), **Lady Luck's Express Buffet** (tel: 477-3000) and the Fremont Hotel's **Paradise Buffet** (tel: 385-34232). **Molly's Buffet** (tel: 388-2400) is the folksiest in town, with country-style fare.

THEME RESTAURANTS

Theme restaurants, which tend to have amusing ambiance, deafening background noise and big tariffs, are proliferating. Examples are the **Harley Davidson Cafe** (opposite the Bellagio, tel: 740-4555); the **Hard Rock Cafe** (Paradise Road at Harmon, tel: 733-7625); **Rainforest Cafe** (inside the MGM Grand, tel: 891-8580) and the **NASCAR Cafe** (2535 Las Vegas Blvd S, tel: 734-7223).

Planet Hollywood
The grand-daddy of Vegas theme restaurants is Planet Hollywood at 3500 Las Vegas Blvd S, tel: 369-6001. As you might expect, this branch of the hamburger chain is also the largest. Diners can gaze at Clint Eastwood's pistol from *A Fistful of Dollars*, Richard Gere's motorcycle from *An Officer and a Gentleman*, and Barbara Eden's genie bottle from TV's *I Dream of Jeannie*.

SHOPPING

CASINO ARCADES

Caesars Palace reputedly spent $100 million creating the **Forum Shops** (tel: 893-4800) arcade adjoining its casino, and readers of the local *Review Journal* have five times nominated it as the best people-watching place in town. The upscale mall averages sales of $1,100 per square ft ($12,000 per square meter) – the highest in the nation. The fake sky overhead evolves from sunrise to sunset every hour or two, and costumed hostesses and gladiators line the marbled halls (for more information *see page 43*).

The adjoining **Appian Way** (tel: 731-7110), marked by a replica of Michelangelo's *David*, is more low-key, with boutiques predominating. A store called Ancient Creations sells one-of-a-kind artifacts ranging from Roman glass to antique jewels.

Halfway along the Forum, the street opens out into a fountain-filled piazza, where talking statues of the gods Plutus, Bacchus and Apollo perform, accompanied by lasers every hour on the hour. Among the restaurants is a branch of Wolfgang Puck's trendy Spago. There is also a large simulated ride in a domed theater using 3-D movies, and with an 82-ft (25-meter) screen, plus an Omnimax Theater (2–10pm Sun–Thur, noon–11pm weekends). Opposite the entrance is the Atlantis Aquarium; tropical fish are fed at 3.15 and 7.15pm.

All the major hotel-casinos have their own shopping arcades, with the **Via Bellagio** (tel: 693-7111) particularly spectacular. Strolling down a lavishly carpeted grand hallway tiled in marble, the visitor can in quick succession pop into Hermès and Prada, browse around Armani and Gucci or checkout the diamond bracelets in Fred Leighton's.

The **Paris Hotel-Casino** has a range of shops on a Parisian theme, selling food, wine and fashion. There have been unconfirmed rumors that a branch of the famed London department store Harrods might open near Mandalay Bay.

Hotel shops sell quality keepsakes that match the house theme. In the better shops, such souvenirs start at around $25 and go up to hundreds of dollars. **Treasure Island** commissioned intricately patterned ceramic platters, bowls and chests inlaid with camel bones for its Loot of Booty shop. At **Excalibur**, the lamps, paintings, sculptures and copies of weaponry come mostly from Spain. **The Mirage** has carved fish from Bali and South Seas totems. **Luxor** gift shops feature hand-tooled leather boxes and glass perfume bottles from Egypt. Its accessories are inspired by the Sphinx.

Nevertheless, T-shirts are the single most popular item at the Luxor's **Giza Galleria** (tel: 262-4000), selling at a rate of 10,000 a month. Typical Las Vegas designs include volcanoes,

---

👁 Bargain entertainment

The concept of window shopping – looking but not necessarily buying – has achieved new dimenisons in Las Vegas, where at least two of the recent malls are so spectacularly entertaining that shoppers are outnumbered by sightseers (a worrying concept for their owners). Desert Passage describes itself as 'the world's most exotic marketplace,' and, in the Venetian's Grand Canal Shoppes, mere shopping can pale next to gondola rides and watching the flocks of pigeons fly on schedule in and out of the Piazza San Marco.

swaying palms and Queen Nefertiti with her jackal Anubis (Luxor); skulls and pirates (Treasure Island); and dragons and charging knights (Excalibur). Some more generic shirts say *To Gamble or Not to Gamble: What a Stupid Question.*

Although almost all the upscale casinos have their own arcades, the smaller casinos aim for the tacky gift rather than the tremendous. **Harrah's** gift store, for example, offers a beer mug that burps.

Miles of aisles

Bonanza, at the corner of the Strip and Sahara Avenue, claims to be the world's largest souvenir store. It sells the sort of inexpensive tokens perfect for friends and family (especially those you don't like). Everything from casino-chip key rings and replicas of Elvis's sunglasses to lime-green garden gnomes fill Bonanza's acres of shelves.

SHOPPING MALLS

The largest selection of stores on the Strip is inside the recently enlarged **Fashion Show Mall**, 3200 Las Vegas Blvd, tel: 369-0704. Stretching a couple of blocks along Spring Mountain Road adjoining the north side of Treasure Island, the mall is anchored by Neiman Marcus, Saks Fifth Avenue and Dillard's. The ongoing expansion (due for completion in 2002) will add Nordstrom, Bloomingdale's and Lord & Taylor. Currently there are 145 shops on two levels, with parking; the mall is open until 9pm on weekdays, and 6pm on weekends.

Nevada's largest, **The Boulevard** mall (Maryland Parkway at Desert Inn, tel: 732-8949), anchored by Sears, Dillard's, Macy's and JC Penny's, is open until 9pm weekdays, until 6pm on Sundays. A close second in size is Henderson's **Galleria Mall**. Shops

selling Western wear can be found in many malls, with Sheplers among the 95 stores in **Sahara Pavilions**, 4760 W Sahara, tel: 258-2000. From the Strip take bus 103 or 204; from Downtown, bus 207.

FACTORY OUTLETS

America's largest factory outlet mall, the **Belz Factory Outlet**, 7400 Las Vegas Blvd S, tel: 896-5599, beyond Mandalay Bay, has 155 outlets and gets 6½ million visitors a year. Ample parking includes a large area for tour buses, and the brochures are printed in five languages.

At least fifty other stores are located in the **Las Vegas Factory Outlet Stores of America** (9115 Las Vegas Blvd S, tel: 817-9090) on the local CAT bus route along the Strip. An upscale and even larger mall, housing names like Escada, Calvin Klein, and Versace is **Fashion Outlet Las Vegas**, 45 minutes away in the town of **Primm**.

Shuttle buses run to Primm from the New York-New York and the MGM Grand casinos (tel: 702 874-1400) and there is also a helicopter service. Allstate Ticketing (tel: 800/634-6787) operates daily tours ($25) of the Fashion Outlet at Primm and the Beltz Factory Outlet, allowing two hours in each place and providing pick-up from individual hotels.

CRAFTS AND SOUVENIRS

Navajo crafts people create attractive goods from gold and silver at **Begay Indian Jewelry** (1311 Nevada Highway, Boulder City, tel: 2293-4822) which is on Highway 95/93 towards Hoover Dam.

At the **Gamblers General Store** (800 S Main St, tel: 800/322-2447) there's a wide selection of modern and antique slot machines, gaming videos and roulette tables.

NIGHTLIFE

The biggest hotels tend to book famous names, while the Flamingo Hilton and the Riviera favor big, splashy shows with lots of chorus girls in scanty costumes. Prices usually include tip and two drinks. The average price for a regular show is around $40–$50, but the top ones, such as the Mirage's **Siegfried & Roy** or anything by **Cirque du Soileil**, can cost more than double that amount. The top shows are extremely popular, so be sure to book way in advance, and plan your visit around them. Slightly less expensive and a good night out is a show by the **Blue Man Group**, now ensconced at the Luxor.

MUSIC

Mandalay Bay's sky-high **House of Blues** is a 1,800-capacity live music venue, with after hours dancing on weekends beginning at 11pm; internationally-known musicians play twice-nightly at the **Blue Note Las Vegas** (tel: 862-8307) and **Très Jazz** (tel: 946-7000) is a Parisian-style supper club tucked away between Paris and Bally's.

Listening to jazz while in a massage chair is the draw at the **Mermaid Cafe & Art Gallery** (2910 E Lake Drive, tel: 240-6002). Downtown's **Four Queens** (tel: 385-4011) has featured Monday Night Jazz since 1981. If you would rather sing than listen, full-on karaoke is the specialty at **Ellis Island** (4178 Koval Lane, tel: 733-8901) and in the Sahara's **NASCAR Cafe** (tel: 734-7223).

CLUBS

Many casinos have clubs with dancing on offer: **Cleopatra's Barge** (tel: 731-7110) is a replica of an Egyptian ship that rocks in water in Caesars Palace; **Ra**, a nightclub at the Luxor (tel: 262-4000); **Club Rio** (tel: 247-7977) has different specialty nights; the Stardust's **Starlight Lounge** (tel: 732-6111), and the **Gold Coast's Dance Hall** (tel: 3677-7111) with big band music are among the best. Free Country and Western dance lessons are on offer at **Sam's Town Western Dance Hall** (on the Boulder Highway, tel: 456-7777). Would-be cowpokes can take a shot at the mechanical bull in **Gilley's Dance Hall** (New Frontier Hotel, tel: 794-8200) which opens at 4pm daily.

Disco-type clubs include **The Beach** (opposite the Convention Center, tel: 731-1925) with two levels of beach decor; **Drai's After Hours** (tel: 737-7111); **Baby's** at the Hard Rock Hotel (tel: 693-5555); **Club Utopia** (on the Strip near Harmon Ave, tel: 736-3105), and MGM Grand's three-level **Studio 54** (tel: 891-7254).

COMEDY

There's a branch of **The Improv** (tel: 369-5111) in Harrah's casino with twice-nightly shows. Other comedy clubs around town include the **Comedy Stop** (tel:739-2222) at the Tropicana; **Second City** (tel: 733-3111) at the Flamingo, and the Naughty Bones Comedy Troupe (tel: 228-7591) at **Bourbon Street**.

Tickets, tickets
To book tickets in advance for major shows and events, contact Allstate Ticketing, tel: 597-5970, www.showtickets. com; Nevada Ticket Services, tel: 597-1587, www.lasvegastickets.com; or Elmore Sports and Event Management, tel: 798-8345 (for high-profile sports events, like boxing).

THINGS TO DO

Many attractions in casinos draw both adults and children and so are perfect for people traveling with kids. At the **Dolphin Habitat** in **The Mirage**, for example, playful dolphins frolic not only for tourists of all ages but also for Nevada schoolchildren. An educational program has been developed, by the dolphins' project staff and Clark County Schools system, which allows students to visit and learn about the animals and the fragility of the planet's marine ecology.

CROWD-PLEASERS FOR KIDS

Most children's attention is caught on their first visit to the Mirage when, while checking in with their parents, they are enraptured by the sight of sharks, rays, puffer fish and other species swimming in the Coral Reef aquarium right behind the registration desk. And they invariably accompany their parents around **Siegfried & Roy's Secret Garden**, admiring tigers in a semi-tropical habitat.

Probably the biggest crowd-pleaser for children is **Treasure Island's pirate battle**, but when Steve Wynn first installed it he declared: 'I'm after adults – a casino is no place for children. I don't want a kiddie park here. The primary pitch is to the parents.'

Some critics of the 'child-friendly' phase that Las Vegas promoted for a year or two agree with those views. Says William Thompson, a University of Nevada professor and a gambling industry expert: 'Now the kids will see that gambling is okay; they'll see it as socially acceptable. We don't tell our kids that dad just dropped $600.' And he adds: 'You'll also get the Home Alone thing – in other words, bring your kids and dump them while you gamble.'

Circus Circus was probably the first to start appealing to children by offering midway (sideshows) and circus acts to entertain them while the parents gambled. Of course it turned out that adults enjoyed the acrobats and the midway almost as much as their kids did, and both are crowded for most of the day, as are the video games and county-fair-style games.

Behind the casino is the big, fun **Adventuredome Theme Park**, with a double-loop roller coaster and a watery ride past life-size dinosaurs and 140-ft (43-meter) sandstone cliffs. With almost 3 million visitors during the year 2000, it is ranked as the 19th most popular theme park in North America. An all-day pass costs from $13–$17, depending on height.

Kids' stuff

Every twelfth visitor to Las Vegas is accompanied by a minor, a ratio that has doubled in the past few years. This wasn't always the case. Until the advent of three new hotels in 1994 with kiddy-style attractions, only 5 percent of visitors were children. Now, although the 'bring your kids' promotions of recent years have been downplayed, there are still plenty of families who do just that – and an increasing number of attractions for the whole family to enjoy.

Parents who would prefer some time off can take advantage of the numerous child-care facilities and programs for children that most resorts offer (ask your hotel concierge). Babysitting is also available. At least three agencies – Vegas Valley Babysitting (871-5161); Nann's & Granny's (364-4700) and Around the Clock Child Care (365-1040) will send baby sitters to your hotel room to look after your offspring for much less than you'll probably lose on the slot machines.

Kids and caution
Casinos face new difficulties in enforcing the law that prohibits children from gambling in this new era of families waltzing *en masse* through the gambling halls. The legal age for gambling in Nevada is still 21. Security guards are supposed to ask for IDs, but many don't. Some gaming places used to allow youths to bet on horse races if they were tall enough to reach the window, but not any more. The casinos have introduced mandatory training programs to help their employees weed out under-age gamblers, many of whom produce fake IDs.

A curfew bars those under 18 from arcades in the area between 10pm and 5am (from midnight on weekends) and requires that security guards be posted in the larger arcades (those with more than 20 coin-operated amusement machines), with surveillance cameras in the smaller ones.

The MGM Grand's amusement center, now renamed the **Park at the MGM Grand**, is a much scaled-down version of its original self and is now open only to private groups (from 50 to 7,000). The hotel retains its Youth Center, however, where kids can be left for the day.

The city's major attractions for young people are probably the various thrill rides, such as the **Canyon Blaster**, which is what Circus Circus calls its double corkscrew roller coaster, and the Stratosphere's **High Roller**, whose passengers can see the sidewalks 1,000 feet (300 meters) below if they're brave enough to look down. Some of the afternoon lounge shows are kid-friendly, especially the various magicians; a particularly good attraction is 'the Birdman,' Joe Krathwohl, who juggles with macaws in three daily shows at the Tropicana.

Boulder Station, on the Boulder Highway located south of town, has

Kids Quest, a gigantic play area for kids aged six weeks to 12 years. There's a play pit near the entrance, within view of the blackjack tables, a movie and video room and computer games. Other casino-hotels off the Strip with licensed child care facilities include **Sam's Town** (Boulder Highway), **Gold Coast** (Flamingo Road), **Santa Fe** (N Rancho Drive) and **Sunset Station** in Henderson.

OTHER ACTIVITIES

Some of these attractions are also suitable for childen:

All-American Sports Park, 121 E Sunset Rd, tel: 798-7777. Rock climbing wall, batting cages, go-karts. Open weekends: Fri 4–10pm, Sat and Sun from noon.

Big Shot & High Roller, Stratosphere, tel: 380-7711. Daredevil rides atop the tower 100 stories above the ground. Daily 10am–1am.

Chinatown Plaza, 4255 Spring Mountain Rd, tel: 221-8448. Shopping plaza, good restaurants and Oriental wedding temple. Call for free shuttle schedule.

Cookies & Crafts, Borders Book Shop, S Decatur Blvd. Demonstrations with snacks. Sat 2pm.

Eiffel Tower, Paris Las Vegas, tel: 946-7000. Glass elevators ascend 50 stories to the top of this replica of the French landmark, offering spectacular views. Daily 10am–1am.

Elephant Castle, 650 W Sunset Rd, Henderson, tel: 566-7600. Museum and gift shop with more than 2,500 elephant motif collectibles.

The Extraterrestrial Highway, Nevada SR 375. A half-day drive from Las Vegas via I-15 and US 93, the road heads to the town of Rachel, an unofficial UFO headquarters.

Fantasy Faire, Excalibur, tel: 597-7777. Movies of runaway trains and out-of-control dune buggies feature in the

Magic Motion Machine Theater, amidst a plethora of video and other games.
Gilcrease Orchards, 7800 N Tenaya Way, tel: 645-1126. Here you can pick a variety of fruit, depending on the season, and visit the animal sanctuary, which is home to birds and other wild animals needing shelter. Open on Sat mornings.
Gondola rides, outside the Venetian. Located in 'St Marks Square'; the rides are so popular that the hotel has had to hire more gondoliers to meet demand.
Guinness World Records Museum, 2780 Las Vegas Blvd, tel: 792-3766. Full-size replicas of strange-but-true items, color videos, assorted displays. Daily 9am–5.30pm.
Houdini's Museum and Magic Shop, the Venetian, tel: 796-0301. Tiny corner with some of the famous magician's fascinating props and letters. Daily 9am–11pm, till midnight Fri and Sat.
Las Vegas Cyber Speedway, Sahara, tel: 737-2471. Virtual reality NASCAR racing in 3-D theater. Open 10am–10pm daily, from 11 on Sat, from noon on Sun.
Las Vegas Mini Grand Prix, 1401 N Rainbow Blvd, tel: 259-7000. Go-

The Las Vegas Motor Speedway has races to thrill most spectators

Karts and other vehicles race on banked track, plus roller coaster and restaurant. Open 10am–10pm, till midnight weekends, closed Mon.
Las Vegas Motor Speedway, 6915 Speedway Blvd, tel: 651-6300. Watch great races by internationally-known drivers. After taking a class at this prestigious driving academy, you can also handle a real racing car.
The Liberace Museum, 1775 East Tropicana, tel: 798-5595. Here are Rolls-Royces covered in mirror tiles, sequined and jeweled costumes, antique pianos, photographs, jewelry, and the recreated office and bedroom from the Palm Springs hacienda of the campy pianist and Vegas performer, who died in 1987, age 68. Daily 10am–5pm, Sun 1–5pm.
Lied Discovery Children's Museum, 833 N Las Vegas Blvd, tel: 382-5437. Interactive arts and science exhibits. Open 10am–5pm Tues–Sun, closed Mon. Crafts materials are available Tues and Thur for adults and children to work on.
Madame Tussaud's, The Venetian, tel: 367-1847. Based on the famous waxworks first opened in London, England, Las Vegas's Tussaud's has more than 100 life-sized touchable and photographable figures. Open daily 11am–7pm.

Magic Motion Film Ride, Excalibur, tel: 597-7777. A simulated ride into a fantasy world; don't forget to keep an eye out for the dragon in the moat. Open 10am–11pm, weekends 9am–midnight.

Manhattan Express, New York-New York, tel: 740-6969. Coney Island-style roller coaster ride in full view of the crowds that gather outside New York-New York casino. Daily 10am–11pm.

Masquerade Village, Rio, tel: 252-7776. Dancers and singers perform free show above the casino floor every two hours from 4pm every day but Tues and Wed. For an extra ten bucks or so, you and your friends can don a costume and join them.

Moonstruck Gallery, 6322 W Sahara Ave, tel: 364-0531. Art and crafts by local, regional and Native American artists. These include fine jewelry and hand-blown glass. Open Tues–Sat, 10am–6pm.

Elvis-A-Rama

Although 'the King' appears everywhere in Vegas, from 'starring' in retro cabaret shows, to performing marriages, to the dozens of impersonators welcoming visitors into off-Strip casinos and Chinese restaurants – including one impressionist who doubles as a men's room attendent dressed in full sideburns and flashy clothes – the best view of Elvis's life can be gleaned from the Elvis-A-Rama museum at 3401 Industrial Road, situated behind the Fashion Show Mall. The museum reveals, in interactive display cases, the singer's career, spanning the 1950s; the Army years; the '60s and Hollywood movie years, with two entire cases reserved for Presley's outrageous clothes from the 1970s. Other exhibits include the famous 1955 Cadillac, a speedboat, and a $75,000 35-carat red ruby ring. A live stage show is included in the cover price. Open daily 10am–7pm, tel: 309-7200.

Movies: The United Artists Showcase Cinema (tel: 740-4511) next to the MGM Grand. Movies are also shown in the Texas, Boulder and Sunset Station casinos.

Open Mike Poetry, Barnes & Noble, Rainbow Blvd. Second Saturday of each month; mainly for teenagers.

Oxygen Bar, Breathe, tel: (888) 382-8612. Branches are in CK2 in the Venetian; Baby's in the Hard Rock; and the House of Blues. Not one for the kids.

Pahrump Valley Winery, tel: 727-6900. Tours, wine tasting, and restaurant. Daily 10am–4.30pm.

Paintball Games, tel: 595-2555 for information. For children 10 years or older; held on Saturdays.

Race for Atlantis, Caesars Palace, tel: 733-9000. An IMAX 3-D chariot race through a mythical realm. Open 10am–11pm Thurs–Sun, till midnight Fri and Sat.

Red Rooster Antique Mall, 307 W Charleston Blvd, tel: 382-5253. A Victorian-era tea room where guests can dress up in hats, feather boas, shawls and antique jewelry for their tea party, during which Patricia Schell describes the correct etiquette. The session lasts almost two hours.

The Rock Tour, tel: 693-5000. Free map at the desk in the Hard Rock Hotel will guide you around 40 years of musical memorabilia.

Star Trek: The Experience, tel: 732-5111. Visit the 24th-century world of Star Trek from the comfort of the Las Vegas Hilton.

Southern Nevada Zoological Park, 1775 N Rancho Dr, tel: 647-4685. Petting zoo, rare species, reptiles and a botanical garden.

Spas: After a hard night at the gaming tables, treat yourself to a massage at one of Vegas's spas. Spas can be found in Caesars Palace, tel: 731-2222; Imperial Palace, tel: 731-3311; MGM

Grand, tel: 891-3077; Riviera, tel: 794-9441; Flamingo, tel: 733-3535; Monte Carlo, tel: 730-7590; New York-New York, tel: 740-6955; Luxor, tel: 730-5720, and the Venetian's renowned Canyon Ranch, tel: 414-5600. All have workout facilities.
Strat-of-Fair, Stratosphere, tel: 380-7777. Amusement park in the Stratosphere Tower with restored 1958 Ferris Wheel. Open daily 10am–1am, till 2am Fri and Sat.
Sunset Stampede, Sam's Town, tel: 456-7777. Free water show with laser lighting daily at 2, 6, 8 and 10pm.
Wet 'N Wild, 2601 Las Vegas Blvd, tel: 765-9700.Water rides, including a spaceship through the Black Hole. Daily 10am–6pm.

TOURS

Nevada Tours and Travel (tel: 888/413-7184) offers a five-hour bus tour of the city at night, which is probably the quickest way to see the most interesting sights if you don't have much time. Seeing the city from the air is an attraction offered by many companies, the most leisurely probably being that of **Las Vegas Airship Tours** (2642 Airport Drive, North Las Vegas, tel: 646-2888), whose nine passenger blimps float gently over the Strip. **Balloon Las Vegas** (tel: 596-7582) follows its sunrise and sunset flights with a champagne celebration.

Sundance Helicopters (265 E Tropicana, tel: 736-0606) flies you to a champagne picnic in the Grand Canyon; or **Papillon Helicopters** (245 E Tropicana, tel: 888/635-7272), or **Maverick Helicopter Tours** (6075 Las Vegas Blvd S tel: 261-0007), who claim to go even deeper into the canyon than the others.

Eagle Canyon and Scenic Airlines (2705 Airport Drive, tel: 800/446-4584) offers aerial views of Hoover Dam, Lake Mead and other places,

Native American sites
Nevada's Indian territory is a checkerboard of various tribal reservations and colonies. For generations, Native Americans etched their stories in the petroglyphs (rock drawings) of the Valley of Fire and other sacred places, maintaining an unbroken strand of history. They chanted songs, weaved baskets, hunted game and fished, gathered the fruits of the desert, and cared for the land. The tribes that dominate the state are the Northern Paiute and Southern Paiute; the Washoe; the Goshute and the Shoshone. The Southern Paiutes occupied southern and eastern Nevada, including Las Vegas and Laughlin.

Southern Nevada has many Native American artifacts, sights and activities. Two of the best are the Valley of Fire and the Lost City Museum, about 1½ hours' drive from Las Vegas *(see page 79)*. The Las Vegas Indian colony is just northwest of the city on Interstate 15; the Moapa reservation and casino is northeast of the city; while the Fort Mojave reservation is south of Laughlin. The Clark County Museum and the Nevada State Museum and Historical Society both contain exhibits.

For more information contact the Las Vegas Indian Center, tel: 647-5842; the Las Vegas Paiute Resort, tel: 658-1400; the Las Vegas Paiute Tribe, tel: 386-3926; or Moapa Tribal Enterprises, tel: 378-5637.

and will arrange pick-up from hotels. Grand Canyon excursions are also offered by **Las Vegas Tours and Travel** (tel: 739-8975), as well as **Rebel Adventure Tours** (713 E Ogden St, tel: 800/817-6789), which promises white-knuckle, white-water rafting and jet skiing, or **Adventure Photo Tours** (tel: 888/363-8687).

Every tour company offers its staple: a one-day bus tour to Hoover Dam with prices from about $35 depending on length. Pick-ups are made at all the

> **I fly, I do**
> Las Vegas Helicopters, located at 3724 Las Vegas Blvd S, tel 736-0013, operates 50 to 100 flights a night over the city. A basic trip lasts four to eight minutes, and costs around $20-$30, but for an extra $10 you can hover over the Downtown area. The company also offers daytime tours of Lake Mead and Hoover Dam. Weddings in the air are particularly popular. Ministers ride in the front next to the pilot, while the bride and groom sit in the back, saying their vows as they hover over their favorite casino.

hotels, where reservations can usually be done via the concierge. **Gray Line**, 4020 E Mountain Road, tel: 384-1234, has one of the largest groups of tours, including all those above and a six-hour city tour, plus Laughlin, Stateline, Hoover Dam, Valley of Fire, Red Rock Canyon, and Death Valley.

Apart from bus tours, Red Rock Canyon can be explored in a variety of ways: on **Cowboy Trail Rides** (tel: 387-2457), especially romantic by night; hiking with guides from **Sky's the Limit** (tel: 363-4533); with **Red Rock Downhill Bike & Hike Tours** (tel: 617-8965); or from the seat of a Harley Davidson from **North American Motorcycle** (4625 E Tropicana Ave, tel: 434-0200).

Sandy Valley Ranch (tel: 877/726-3998) is where you can spend four or five days learning the ins and outs of roping steers, as well as taking part in barn dances, barbecue dinners and story telling around moonlight campfires. **Bunk Out West** (tel: 888/837-2382) accommodates groups of up to 16 people who are transported out to a working ranch near Ely, where, for five days or more, participants enjoy horsemanship classes, hay rides, cave exploring and nightly poker games. **Annie Bananie's Wild West Tours**

(tel: 804-9755) runs six-hour tours to the Valley of Fire and Lake Mead on Tuesdays, Thursdays and Saturdays. **Desert Odyssey Tours** (tel: 837-7552) also specializes in Valley of Fire Tours, while **Desert Eco-Tours** (1775 N Rancho Dr, tel: 647-4685) operates pricey tours run by trained naturalists.

Lake Mead Cruises (tel: 293-6180) take place on the Desert Princess, a three-deck sternwheeler. You can rent a houseboat to stay on Lake Mead or Lake Mojave from **Forever Resorts** (tel: 800/255-5561). Black Canyon, at the base of Hoover Dam, is the home of **River Raft Tours** (1297 Nevada Highway, Boulder City, tel: 800/696-7238) which picks up at Las Vegas hotels and offers tours along the Colorado River. The company's largest raft seats 42 passengers for its three-hour trips.

Similar excursions are organized by **ATV Action Tours** (175 Cassia Way, Henderson, tel: 888/288-5200). **Creative Adventures Ltd,** PO Box 94043, 361-5565, provides guides specializing in the history, wildlife, vegetation and geology of deserts and canyons.

ACTIVE PURSUITS

The major motels and hotels offer many facilities, usually free to residents; most have swimming pools.
Ballooning: Balloon Las Vegas, 4616 W Sahara Ave, No. 274, tel: 596-7582, offers sunrise and sunset flights daily.
Bicycling: Downhill Bicycling Tours, 7934 Cadenza Lane, tel: 897-8287. Tours of Vegas and out into the desert.
Boating: Willow Beach Harbor, tel: 520/767-4747. The Marina, on Lake Mojave, is located 15 minutes' from Hoover Dam.
Bowling: Alleys include the Gold Coast, 4000 W Flamingo Rd at Valley View, tel: 367-7111; Santa Fe, 4949 N Rancho, tel: 658-4995; and the Castaways, 2800 Fremont St, tel: 385-

9153. All are open 24 hours every day.

Bungy jumping: AJ Hackett Bungy Site, 810 Circus Circus Drive, tel: 385-44321. Freefall jumps from 175-ft (50-meter) atop the world's tallest double-jump platform. Open daily.

Fishing: Las Vegas Bay Marina, Henderson, tel: 565-9111. Good for fisherpersons of all ages.

Flying: North American Top Gun, Boulder City Airport, tel: 888/535-9992, allows you to take part in simulated dogfights while flying a WW2 vintage plane along with an instructor.

Gliding: Las Vegas Soaring Center, Jean Airport, tel: 874-1010. Enjoy a gliding experience, alone or accompanied. Daily 10am–dusk.

Golf: Public courses: Craig Ranch, 628 W Craig Rd, tel: 642-9700; Las Vegas Municipal Course, Decatur and Washington Blvds, tel: 646-3003. Private courses: Las Vegas National Golf Club, 1911 E Desert Inn Rd, tel: 734-1796; Rhodes Ranch Country Club, 7881 S Durango Dr, tel: 270-4665; Dragonride Golf Club, Henderson, tel: 614-4444; and Summerlin Course, 9201 Del Webb Dr, tel: 363-4373.

Hiking: Hiking Tours, Henderson, tel: 5967-2953. Hike the desert.

Rafting in the Black Canyon is a popular pastime

Horseback Riding: Mt Charleston Riding Stables, tel: 872-5408; and Bonnie Springs Old Nevada, Red Rock Canyon, tel: 875-4191.

Racquetball: the Las Vegas Athletic Club, 1070 E Sahara, tel: 734-8944, and Caesars Palace, tel: 731-7110, have racquetball courts.

Skydiving: for simulated flying, try Flyaway Indoor Skydiving, 200 Convention Center Drive, tel: 731-4768. Safety training followed by free-fall simulation inside a 21-ft (6-meter) vertical tunnel. For the real thing, Skydive Las Vegas Inc, Boulder City airport 800/U-SKYDIV, allows you to freefall at 120mph (190 kph) for 46 seconds, harnessed to an instructor, after a 40-minute lesson.

Snow Skiing: Lee Canyon, tel: 593-9500. The lodge is open from the end of November to Easter.

Tennis: Illuminated courts at the YMCA (4141 Meadows Lane, tel: 877-9622) are open weekdays until 10pm, until early evening weekends; similarly inexpensive are the 12 courts on the UNLV campus (Swenson and Harmon, tel: 895-4498). Lorenzi Park (3075 W Washington, tel: 229-4867) has eight illuminated courts. There are seven indoor courts at Bally's casino; six at the Las Vegas Hilton, and four at the Monte Carlo.

PRACTICAL INFORMATION

Getting There

BY PLANE

McCarran International Airport, the 7th busiest in the world, is 1 mile (1.6 km) from the Strip, 5 miles (8 km) from Downtown. There are 700 flights daily and direct connections to 50 US cities. To the airport from the Strip costs around $8 by taxi, $5 by shuttle; from Downtown about $18 by taxi, about $5 by shuttle.

BY CAR

The main route through Las Vegas is Interstate 15 from southern California to Utah and Salt Lake City. From the northwest, US 95 bypasses the city, heading southeast to join Interstate 40 at Needles. From the east, US 70 intersects US 15 about 250 miles (400 km) northeast of Las Vegas.

BY TRAIN

Rail services to Las Vegas ceased in the early 1990s. The nearest railroad station is now at Bakersfield, from which buses connect, although AMTRAK is rumored to be planning a resumption of services from Los Angeles.

What to bring

A whopping 74 percent of visitors to Las Vegas have been to Sin City at least one time before, a repeat-rate that is the envy of countries around the world. The 24 percent of first-time visitors will want to pack sunscreen, sunglasses, a bathing suit and – most importantly – trainers or good walking shoes. Distances in Vegas are hugely deceptive, a casino 'just across the street' can take half an hour in blazing sun to reach. Although it's pleasant to dress up for shows or a fancy dinner, casual dress is tolerated in most of the city's casinos and restaurants.

BY BUS

Greyhound Bus Lines, 200 Main Street, tel: 800-231-2222, connects with all parts of the US. Travelers from the West Coast should ask about the Special Casino Runs at reduced fares. It takes 7 hours to reach Los Angeles; buses leave at 12.30am, 6.40am, 8.10am, noon, 3.15pm and 5.35pm.

Getting Around

A trolley runs along the Strip every 15–20 minutes until 2am, stopping at all major locations. The CAT bus 301 runs from Downtown to the Strip every 10–20 minutes, 24 hours a day. The one-way fare is $2.

Limousines are available with driver from $40 per hour. Taxis: Union, tel: 736-8444; Ace, tel: 736-8383; Checker, tel: 873-2000; Henderson, tel: 384-2322; Star, tel: 873-2000; Western, tel: 736-8000; Whittlesea, tel: 384-6111; Yellow, tel: 873-2000.

Almost all hotels have large free parking lots and also offer valet service at the front entrance.

BIKE AND CAR RENTAL

Dollar Rent A Car, tel: 739-8408 or 800-826-9911; Allstate, tel: 736-6147; Budget, tel: 736-1212; Payless, tel: 736-6147; National, tel: 261-5391; Thrifty, tel: 896-7600; Dream Car Rentals, tel: 731-6452.

Harley Davidson motorcycles can be rented from North American, 434-0200 or Eaglender, (888) 916-7433. There's also Las Vegas Scooters, 3735 Las Vegas Blvd S, tel: 736-8633. The desert is a perfect place to try out the 'hogs,' especially for novice riders.

TOURS

See page 107.

Facts for the Visitor

TRAVEL DOCUMENTS

To enter the US you need a valid passport. Except Canadians, most visitors planning to stay more than 90 days need visas. Vaccinations are not required for entry.

CUSTOMS

If you are 21 or over, you can take into the US 200 cigarettes, 50 cigars, or 3 lb (about 1.4 kg) of tobacco; 1 US quart of alcohol (about 0.9 liters); and duty free gifts worth up to $100. You are not allowed to bring in meat products, seeds, plants or fruits. You can take out anything.

> **Dialing codes**
> All of Las Vegas, and most of Nevada, is in the 702 zone. If no preceding number is given in this book, dial 702 if calling Las Vegas from out of state.

TOURIST INFORMATION/WEBSITES

Las Vegas Convention & Visitors Authority, 3150 Paradise Rd, Las Vegas, tel: 892-7575, fax: 892-7553 or www.lv24hours.com. Other good websites include www.vegas. com for attractions, and www.lvchamber.com for events and local news.

ALCOHOL/TOBACCO

You must be over 21 to drink legally; there are no closing hours for purchase or consumption. 'No smoking' signs are practically unheard of *(see page 70)*, but the Mirage and Bellagio have banned smoking in their poker rooms, where high rollers tend to spend hours.

CLIMATE

Las Vegas is hot and arid. The average temperature in the city is about 66°F (19°C) with an average annual rainfall of 4.2 inches (10.6 cm).

Summer temperatures average just below 70°F (21°C) over 24 hours, and the average winter temperature is 48°F (9°C). July and August are very hot, reaching 100°F (38°C).

In October, the days are balmy but nights start to grow cool. Some outdoor swimming pools close, although all but about 50 days of the year are fine for sunbathing. In November, daytime temperatures drop below 70°F (21°C) and nights are cold until April.

CURRENCY/EXCHANGE

The unit of currency in the US is the dollar ($), made up of 100 cents (¢). Major hotels will change foreign currency, but you usually get a better rate from American Express in the MGM Grand, tel: 739-8474, and American Foreign Exchange in the Las Vegas Hilton, tel: 892-0100. The ATMs in the casinos charge $1–2 per transaction.

GAMBLING HELP

Some people gamble unwisely and get in over their heads, and for them help is just the proverbial phone call away. Sponsored jointly by the Nevada Resort Association and the Nevada Council on Problem Gambling, trained counselors stand by 24 hours a day at (800) 522-4700. All calls are completely confidential.

MEDIA

Las Vegas has two daily papers, the *Las Vegas Review Journal* and the *Las Vegas Sun*. There are seven television stations and 30 radio stations. The *Las Vegas Advisor* – detailing the best on offer in Las Vegas – can be ordered on subscription from Huntingdon Press, tel: 800-244-2224.

MEDICAL ASSISTANCE

There is a Medical Clinic, tel: 735-3600, on the 8th floor of the Imperial Palace Hotel. It is open daily, 24 hours, and no appointment is necessary. There are two other 24-hour medical services: (800)-DOCS-911 and 735-3600. Nearby are the Summerlin Hospital Medical Center (tel: 283-7000), the Boulder City Hospital (tel: 293-4111) and Lake Mead Hospital (tel: 649-7711).

OPENING TIMES

Las Vegas is a 24-hour city. The casinos are open 24 hours, as are many service stores, supermarkets etc. Banks usually keep business hours of 9am–3pm weekdays and one evening until 6pm. Post Offices open 9am–6pm weekdays, 8am–noon on Saturday.

PUBLIC HOLIDAYS

New Year's Day (January 1); Martin Luther King Day (3rd Monday in January); Washington's Birthday (3rd Monday in February); Memorial Day (last Monday in May); Independence Day (July 4); Labor Day (1st Monday in September); Columbus Day (2nd Monday in October); Veterans' Day (November 11); Thanksgiving (4th Thursday in November); Christmas Day (December 25). Most casinos stay open every day of the year.

SECURITY

While you are more likely to be robbed of your money by legitimate means, you should be aware of pickpockets in Las Vegas. Guards are ubiquitous in all the casinos, and they will happily provide an escort on hotel property. However, gamblers are warned to keep an eye on their belongings. 'Guests should always be aware of who is playing next to them,' one security chief warns.

Waist packs and money belts are safer than wallets and purses, as some thieves specialize in distracting people's attention. For example, never place buckets of coins between the

machines where they can be swiftly grabbed when your attention is drawn to the sound of coins hitting the floor.

TELEPHONE

Local calls are free; calls from a coin box cost 35¢. If you act as if you belong, you might be able to score free calls from certain gaming rooms. For local information, tel: 411. For 800 and 1-877 numbers (free calls), tel: 1-800-555-1212.

TIME

Most of Nevada, like the state of California, is in the Pacific Time Zone – two hours behind Chicago, three hours behind New York and eight hours behind London.

TIPPING

Amid so much money changing hands, expectations are, of course, high. Most waiters and waitresses anticipate 15–20 percent tips, with bartenders getting $1 per round from twosomes or small groups. A dollar bill is the usual perk for almost all minor services. Croupiers expect the occasional *baksheesh*, naturally, and it's customary to tip whoever provided the loose change when a slot machine pays off. Hotel maids expect $1 per day at the end of the visit, and pool attendants get about $1. Taxi drivers expect at least $1–2, valet parking attendants $1–2.

VOLTAGE

Standard voltage is 110 volts AC, and adapters are necessary for appliances rated for 220–240 V.

WEDDINGS

An average of 280 weddings a day are performed in Las Vegas, mainly because nothing is needed except a license. Pick one up from 200 S 3rd Street, tel: 455-4416, between 8am and midnight.

WHERE TO STAY

Before deciding where to stay in Las Vegas, it's best to decide whether you are going to gamble. If you are, you can get favorable terms at many casinos because they expect to win some of your money. If you're likely to be a big spender, you may even be 'RFB comped' – which means complimentary room, food and beverage.

The reason why hotel rooms are so cheap in Las Vegas is that the people in an average room generate $80 a day for the casino, and the cost of daily maintenance is about $20 a room. So even if a casino gives a room away at $20 a night it has covered its costs. Any other non-gaming city has only its room rate and food and beverage to make up the revenue.

If you are planning to spend time playing slot machines at such older hotels as the Riviera, Stardust, Sahara or Westward Ho, you should inquire about joining the casino's slot club. Usually they'll issue you with a credit card that operates the machines, and one of the benefits is a good room rate.

You also have to decide between the Strip (in the thick of things), somewhere quieter, or Downtown. Should you decide to stay in one of the swanky hotel-casinos, remember that rates vary tremendously, and at weekends, holidays and during big conventions the prices shoot up. The bigger hotels – the Bellagio, MGM Grand, New York-New York, Venetian – tend to be the most expensive, but ask for the dates you plan to visit and there may be a bargain break on offer.

Among the big-name hotel-casinos, Caesars Palace quotes single or double rooms for around $125 on its rate card, which suggests a pretty constant rate. Circus Circus occasionally advertises rooms for as low as $20 a person.

THE STRIP
Here is a list of hotels and casino-hotels on or near the Strip:

Aladdin Resort and Casino
3667 Las Vegas Blvd S
Tel: (702) 785-5555 or
(877) 333-WISH
Fax: (702) 736-7107
www.aladdincasino.com

Bally's Las Vegas
3645 Las Vegas Blvd S
Tel: (702) 739-4111 or
(800) 634-3434
Fax: (702) 967-4405
www.ballyslv.com

Barbary Coast
3595 Las Vegas Blvd S
Tel: (702) 737-7111 or
(888) 227-2279
Fax: (702) 894-9954
www.barbarycoastcasino.com

Bellagio
3600 Las Vegas Blvd S
Tel: (702) 693-7111 or
(888) 987-6667
Fax: (702) 792-7646
www.bellagiolasvegas.com

Boardwalk Casino-Holiday Inn
3750 Las Vegas Blvd S

10 out of 10
According to a recent survey, Las Vegas has all of the 10 largest hotels in the United States. These are:

MGM Grand	5,034 rooms
The Luxor	4,407 rooms
The Excalibur	4,008 rooms
Circus Circus	3,770 rooms
The Flamingo	3,642 rooms
Mandalay Bay	3,221 rooms
Las Vegas Hilton	3,174 rooms
The Mirage	3,004 rooms
The Venetian	3,036 rooms
The Bellagio	3,005 rooms

Rooms on the web
You can book hotel rooms on-line with the following companies:

www.travelworm. com
www.destinationlasvegas. com
www.lvtb.com (Las Vegas Tourist Bureau)
www.800govgas.
www.hoteldiscount. com

Most of these companies also operate a booking service by telephone.

Tel: (702) 735-2400 or
(800) 635-4581
Fax: (702) 739-8152
www.hiboardwalk.com

Caesars Palace
3570 Las Vegas Blvd S
Tel: (702) 731-7110 or
(800) 634-6661
Fax: (702) 731-7172
www.caesars.com

Circus Circus
2880 Las Vegas Blvd S
Tel: (702) 734-0410 or
(800) 444-2472
Fax: (702) 734-5897
www.circuscircus.com

Club de Soleil
5499 W Tropicana Ave
Tel: (702) 221-0400 or 877-4-SOLEIL
Fax: (702) 579-9120
www.clubdesoleil.com

Convention Center Courtyard by Marriott
3275 Paradise Rd
Tel: (702) 791-3600 or
(800) 321-2220
Fax: (702) 796-7981
www.marriott.com

Crowne Plaza Las Vegas
4255 S Paradise Rd.
Tel: (702) 369-4400 or
800-2-CROWNE
Fax: (702) 369-3770
www.sixcontinentshotels.com

Embassy Suites Convention Center
3600 Paradise Rd
Tel: (702) 893-8000 or
(800)-EMBASSY
Fax: (702) 893-0378
www.embassysuites.com

Embassy Suites Las Vegas
4315 Swenson St
Tel: (702) 795-2800 or
800-EMBASSY
Fax: (702) 795-1520
www.embassylasvegas.com

Emerald Springs-Holiday Inn
325 E Flamingo Rd
Tel: (702) 732-9100 or
(800) 732-7889
Fax: (702) 731-9784
www.holidayinnlasvegas.com

Excalibur
3850 Las Vegas Blvd S
Tel: (702) 597-7777 or
(800) 937-7777
Fax: (702) 597-7009
www.excaliburcasino.com

Flamingo Las Vegas
3555 Las Vegas Blvd S
Tel: (702) 733-3111 or
(800) 732-2111
Fax: (702) 733-3353
www.flamingolasvegas.com

Four Seasons
3960 Las Vegas Blvd S
Tel: (702) 632-5000 or
(877) 632-5000
Fax: (702) 632-5195
www.fourseasons.com

Hard Rock
4455 Paradise Rd
Tel: (702) 693-5000 or
(800) 693-7625
Fax: (702) 693-5010
www.hardrockhotel.com

Harrah's
3475 Las Vegas Blvd S
Tel: (702) 369-5000 or
800-HARRAHS

Hotel San Remo
115 E Tropicana
Tel: (702) 739-9000 or

(800) 522-7366
Fax: (702) 736-1120
www.sanremolasvegas.com
Imperial Palace
3535 Las Vegas Blvd S
Tel: (702) 731-3311 or
(800) 634-6441
Fax: (702) 735-8578
www.imperialpalace.com
Las Vegas Hilton
3000 Paradise Rd
Tel: (702) 732-5111 or
(800) 732-7117
Fax: (702) 794-3611
www.lv-hilton.com
Luxor
3900 Las Vegas Blvd S
Tel: (702) 262-4000 or
(800) 288-1000
Fax: (702) 262-4404
www.luxor.com
Mandalay Bay
3950 Las Vegas Blvd S
Tel: (702) 632-7777 or
(877) 632-7000
Fax: (702) 632-7108
www.mandalaybay.com
MGM Grand
3799 Las Vegas Blvd S
Tel: (702) 891-7777 or
(800) 929-1111

Las Vegas's hotels represent very good value for money

Fax: (702) 891-1030
www.mgmgrand.com
The Mirage
3400 Las Vegas Blvd S
Tel: (702) 791-7111 or
(800) 627-6667
Fax: (702) 791-7414
www.mirage.com
Monte Carlo
3770 Las Vegas Blvd S
Tel: (702) 730-7777 or
(800) 311-8999
Fax: (702) 730-7250
www.monte-carlo.com
The New Frontier
3120 Las Vegas Blvd S
Tel: (702) 794-8200 or
(800) 421-7806
Fax: (702) 794-8445
www.frontierlv.com
New York-New York
3790 Las Vegas Blvd S
Tel: (702) 740-6969 or
(800) 693-6763
Fax: (702) 740-6920
www.nynyhotelcasino.com
The Orleans Hotel
4500 W Tropicana Ave
Tel: (702) 365-7111 or
(800) 675-3267
www.orleanscasino.com
Paris Las Vegas
3655 Las Vegas Blvd S
Tel: (702) 946-7000 or

(888) 266-5687
Fax: (702) 946-4405
www.paris-lv.com
Polo Towers
3745 Las Vegas Blvd S
Tel: (702) 261-1000 or
(800) 935-2233
Fax: (702) 261-1020
www.polotowers.com

NEAR THE STRIP

Here is a list of motels near the Strip:
The Carriage House
105 E Harmon Ave
Tel: 798-1020 or (800) 221-2301
Fax: 798-1020
www.carriagehouselasvegas.com
Suites with kitchenettes, pool,
whirlpool, sports court, free shuttle. **$$**
Doubletree Club
7250 Pollock Drive
Tel: 948-4000 or (800) 222-TREE
Fax: 948-4100
www.doubletree.com
Non-gaming hotel with free shuttle to
Strip and airport. Fitness center, pool,
bakery cafe. **$–$$**
Fairfield Inn
3850 Paradise Rd
Tel: 791–0899 or 800 228-2800
Fax: 791-2705
Airport shuttle, free breakfast, pool,
jacuzzi. **$–$$**
Hampton Inn Tropicana

> ### Hotel price guide
> Room rates vary so much according
> to season that specific estimates are
> hard to forecast. Usually, it is possible at almost
> any time and almost anywhere (except the lux-
> ury hotel/casinos) to book a double room for
> under $100. Often, there is little difference in
> price between a single and a double room.
>
> **$ = under $100**
> **$$ = $100–$150**
> **$$$ = $150 upward**

4975 Industrial Road
Tel: 948-8100 or (877) LV-HOTEL
Fax: 948-8101
Across the freeway, 10 blocks from
the Strip. Pool, fitness center,
free airport and casino shuttle, laun-
dromat. **$–$$**
Hawthorne Inn & Suites
4975 S Valley View Blvd
Tel: 798-7736
Fax: 798-5951
Non-gaming hotel. Theme suites,
pool, exercise facility, pets allowed.
$$
Key Largo
377 E Flamingo Rd
Tel: 733-7777 or (800) 634-6617
Fax: 734-5071
www.keylargocasino.com
Pool, jacuzzi, wedding gazebo, rooms
with refrigerators. **$**
King Albert Motel
185 Albert Ave
Tel: (702) 732-1555 or
(800) 553-7753
Pool, kitchenettes, laundromat, very
inexpensive. **$**
Howard Johnson/Days Inn
5100 Paradise Rd
Tel: 798-2777 or 800-634-6439
Fax: 736-8295
Free shuttle service to airport. **$**
Motel 6
195 E Tropicana Ave
Tel: (702) 798-0728
Three blocks from the Strip, near the
airport. Pool, parking, food shop. **$**
Motel 8
3961 Las Vegas Blvd S
Tel: (702) 798-7223
Opposite Mandalay Bay. Inexpensive
and perfectly acceptable. **$**
Rodeway Inn and Suites
167 E Tropicana
Tel: (702) 795-3311 or (800) 228-2000
Fax: 795-7333
Adjoins Motel 6. Pool, laundromat,
children free with parents, restaurant
next door. **$**

DOWNTOWN

Here is a list of hotels and motels located in or near the downtown area: The fringes of the downtown area can be a hazardous place in which to be alone at night, so it's advisable to stay close to Fremont Street where there are plenty of people around.

California Hotel
12 Ogden
Tel: 385-1222 or (800) 634-6505
Fax 388-2610
www.thecal.com
Attractive Hawaiian decor. Popular with Asian visitors. **$**

City Center Motel
700 Fremont
Tel: 383-4766
Fax: 384-8471
Pool, sun deck, 58 rooms, restaurant opposite. **$**

Days Inn
Fremont & 7th Streets
Tel: 386-1400 or (800) 323-2344
Fax: 388-8622
Motel chain. Pool, restaurant. **$**

Downtowner Motel
129 N 8th St
Tel: 384-1441 or (800) 777-2566
Fax 384-2308
Kitchenettes, free donuts, coffee. **$**

El Cortez
600 E Fremont
Tel: 385-5200 or 800/634-6703
Fax: 385-1554
308 rooms. **$–$$**

Four Queens
202 Fremont
Tel: 387 5102 or (800) 634-6045
www.fourqueens.com
One of the best-known casinos and hotels in the area; 690 rooms. **$$**

Golden Gate Hotel
1 Fremont Street
Tel: 385-1906 or (800) 26-1906
Fax: 383-9681
The city's oldest hotel. Built in 1906 and refurbished in 1930s San Francisco style. **$**

> ### What's in an average?
> According to the Las Vegas News Bureau, the average rate for a non-casino hotel room is around $70 a night, regardless of whether it is occupied by one or two people. These prices are set to rise, however, as an 'energy surcharge' is passed on to visitors to offset the escalating price of electricity. Always ask, when booking, what the taxes on top of the basic rate will be.

Golden Inn Motel
120 Las Vegas Blvd N
Tel: 384-8204
Only one block below Fremont Street, right at Ogden Avenue. **$**

Golden Nugget
129 E Fremont
Tel: 385 7111 or (800) 634-3454
Fax: 386-8632
www.goldennugget.com
This famous hotel and casino gets an AAA 4-diamond rating. **$–$$**

Las Vegas Backpackers
1322 Fremont St
Tel: 385-1150 or (800) 550-8958
Fax: 385-4940
www.hostels.com/lvbackpacker
Cheap accommodations in the downtown area. Free pick-up from Greyhound, pool, jacuzzi. **$**

Main Street Station
200 N Main St
Tel: (702) 387-1896 or
(800) 465-0711
Victorian-style interior. Microbrewery and garden buffet. **$**

Plaza Hotel
1 Main Street
Tel: 386-2110, or (800) 634-6575
Fax: 383-8281
email: plazahotelcasino.com
This is the tallest and biggest Downtown hotel, with 1,000 rooms. Located right next to the Greyhound bus station. Pool, fitness center with jogging track, tennis courts, restaurant. **$–$$**

OTHER HOTELS AND MOTELS

Even on the Strip there are a few non-hectic places. Try **La Concha**, 2955 Las Vegas Blvd, tel: 735-1255, fax: 369-0862, which sits quietly opposite the Stardust. Rooms cost around $50 during the week, up to $75 at weekends, and a little more during holidays and conventions. Also relatively quiet is **the Algiers**, centrally located between Circus Circus and Convention Center Drive, with a pleasant patio café beside a huge swimming pool.

Nearer to the airport and the Strip are the chain motels: **Rodeway Inn, Motel 6**, and **Howard Johnson/Days Inn**. Nearest to Downtown (without actually being in Downtown) are a string of perfectly acceptable, inexpensive motels at the northern end of Las Vegas Boulevard, such as the **Econo Lodge** (1150 Las Vegas Blvd, tel: 800/553-2666); the **Oasis Motel** (1731 Las Vegas Blvd, tel: 735-6494); and the **Rummel Motel** (1809 Las Vegas Blvd, tel: 731-5152).

OUT OF TOWN

Henderson and Boulder City

Hyatt Regency-Lake Las Vegas Resort
101 Montelago Blvd, Henderson
Tel: 562-1234 or (800) 55-HYATT
Fax: 567-6112
www.lakelasvegas.hyatt.com
Sprawling desert resort with golf course on lake. **$$**

The Reserve Hotel Casino
777 Lake Mead Drive, Henderson
Tel: 558-7000 or (800) 899-7770
Fax: 567-7809
www.ameristars.com
African safari theme resort, 20 mins from the Strip. Pool, restaurants. **$$**

Lake Mead Resort
322 Lakeshore Road, Boulder City
Tel: 293-2074 or (800) PLAY-NOW
Fax: 293-7017
www.sevencrown.com

Quiet, restful lakeview lodge with floating restaurant. Pool. **$$**

Lake Mead Houseboats
Callville Marina & Echo Bay
Tel: (800) 225-5561 or (800) 752-9669
On the water, 45 minutes from the Strip. Boats sleep up to 10 people. Rentals from three days to up to seven days. **$–$$**

Boulder Oaks RV Resort
1010 Industrial Road, Boulder City
Tel: 294-4425 or (800) 478-5687
Attractive clubhouse overlooking Lake Mead, pool, laundromat, fishing, golf and tennis. **$**

Laughlin

Bay Shore Inn
1955 W Casino Drive
Tel: 299-9010
Fax: 299-9194
Pool, spa, some kitchenettes, small pets allowed. **$**

Colorado Belle
2100 S Casino Drive
Tel: 298-4000 or (800) 47-RIVER
Fax: 299-0669
www.coloradobelle.com
The Belle contains Laughlin's only microbrewery. **$**

Pioneer Hotel & Gambling Hall
2200 S Casino Drive
Tel: 298-2442 or (800)634-3469
Fax: 298-7462
www.santafegaming.com/pio
Olde West-style motel with mock gun-fights on weekends. **$**

Overton

Best Western North Shore Inn
520 Moapa Valley Blvd, Overton
Tel: (702) 397-6000 or
(800) 528-1234
Fax: 397-6008
Overton is a short drive from the spectacular Valley of Fire. Pool, free breakfast and nearby restaurants. **$**

Opposite: waiting for the show